LIVE FULLY.
LEAVE WISELY.

END-OF-LIFE PLANNING AS THE ULTIMATE ACT OF LOVE

PAUL FRIED

Live Fully. Leave Wisely.
Copyright © 2025 by Paul Fried.

All rights reserved. No part of this publication may be reproduced, distributed, or transmitted in any form or by any means, including photocopying, recording, or other electronic or mechanical methods, without the written consent of the publisher. The only exceptions are for brief quotations included in critical reviews and other noncommercial uses permitted by copyright law.

MILTON & HUGO L.L.C.
4407 Park Ave., Suite 5
Union City, NJ 07087, USA

Website: *www. miltonandhugo.com*
Hotline: *1- 888-778-0033*
Email: *info@miltonandhugo.com*

Ordering Information:
Quantity sales. Special discounts are granted to corporations, associations, and other organizations. For more information on these discounts, please reach out to the publisher using the contact information provided above.

Library of Congress Control Number:	2025920915	
ISBN-13:	979-8-89285-708-6	[Paperback Edition]
	979-8-89285-709-3	[Hardback Edition]
	979-8-89285-710-9	[Digital Edition]

Rev. date: 11/12/2025

DEDICATION

To my father, **Eugene Fried**

A man who faced death over and over in the most horrific ways,

who endured loss no one should ever know,

and yet chose to live with humility, love, and gratitude.

Your strength and your grace continue to guide me.

This book is for you.

CONTENTS

Dedication v
Introduction ix
Chapter 1   The Great Avoidance 1
   How denial of death leaves us unprepared for life's end.

Chapter 2   The Unspoken Weight 7
   The burden silence places on families in times of loss.

Chapter 3   The Fragile Illusion Of Control 13
   Why accepting mortality frees us to live fully.

Chapter 4   When Silence Hurts 19
   How daily choices shape the story we leave behind.

Chapter 5   The Stories We Leave Behind 24
   Why grief should be embraced rather than hidden.

Chapter 6   Health Care Decisions 30
   Clarity and dignity in choosing care when you cannot speak.

Chapter 7   Beyond Legalities 36
   End-of-life planning as an act of love, not paperwork.

Chapter 8   Grief As Love 42
   How grief reflects the depth of our connections.

Chapter 9   Reducing The Stress 48
   Planning ahead to ease the burdens left to others.

Chapter 10   Conversations That Matter 53
   The importance of open dialogue about death and wishes.

Chapter 11 Starting Small 58
   Taking simple steps to begin preparing with clarity.

Chapter 12 Keeping It Simple 63
   Why planning does not need to be overwhelming.

Chapter 13 Updating The Plan 69
   Adapting decisions as life circumstances change.

Chapter 14 The Business Of Death 75
   Understanding how the industry shapes choices.

Chapter 15 The Digital Afterlife.. 81
   Preparing for the legacy we leave online.

Chapter 16 Planning Across Cultures And Faiths 87
   Learning from diverse traditions about life and death.

Chapter 17 Conversations With Children 93
   Helping young people understand death with honesty.

Chapter 18 Planning For Caregivers..................................... 98
   Easing the burden on those who give care.

Chapter 19 Green And Alternative Burials 104
   Exploring environmentally conscious ways to be remembered.

Chapter 20 Your Legacy In Action 110
   Living today in ways that shape tomorrow's memory.

Chapter 21 The Beginning Of Legacy.................................117
   The plans you make may end with your life, but your legacy begins with how you live.

Epilogue 123
About the Author... 125

INTRODUCTION

Why Talk About Death?

We spend much of our lives pretending that death is far away, something that belongs to other people, something that can be kept at bay with good health, busy schedules, and hopeful denial. We bury it under distractions, soften it with gentle words, and try to disguise it with rituals that make it look less frightening. Yet the truth remains. Pretending death isn't coming does not make it disappear. It only makes it harder when it arrives.

And it always arrives.

When it does, families are often left scrambling. In the middle of their grief, they are forced to face a flood of questions. Did Mom want to be buried or cremated. Did Dad have a will. Who should speak at the service. How much will this cost, and who will pay for it. Grief is already heavy enough without the additional weight of confusion, conflict, and chaos piled on top. I have seen families fracture under that weight, not because they did not love each other, but because no one had taken the time to write down the simplest of plans.

That reality is what led me to create I Made the Arrangements, a platform built to make planning accessible, compassionate, and deeply human. Through this work, I have witnessed what happens when families are prepared and what happens when they are not. I have seen grief expressed purely as love, when clarity allowed people to focus on memories instead of logistics. And I have seen grief buried under paperwork, debt, and arguments that never should have existed. The difference is not in how much people loved one another. The difference is whether someone had the courage to prepare.

This book is not about morbidity. It is about love. It is about courage. It is about facing the one thing we cannot escape so that we can live more fully today and leave peace behind tomorrow. The message I want you to carry into every page is simple. Any plan is better than no plan.

When you take even the smallest step, writing down a single wish, naming one person to speak for you, you give your loved ones a priceless gift. You remove the heavy burden of guessing. You free them from the guilt of wondering if they did the right thing. You give them the space to grieve honestly, without the shadow of conflict. You give them clarity. You give them peace.

That is love in its purest form. Not in flowers or gifts or grand gestures, but in the quiet, thoughtful act of making sure the people you leave behind are protected. That is what it means to live fully and leave wisely.

My mission, through this book and through I Made the Arrangements at www.imadethearrangements.com

Chapter

1

THE GREAT AVOIDANCE

In America, death is the quietest guest at the table. We'll argue about politics until we're red in the face, gossip about neighbors, talk money, health, even sex, but when the word death enters the room, the air changes. Forks pause midair. Eyes drop to plates. Someone coughs and changes the subject. We live in a culture where almost anything can be discussed, dissected, and debated, yet death is still treated as a profanity, not obscene because it shocks, but obscene because it cannot be negotiated. It refuses to play by the rules we've built our lives around.

So we soften it, disguise it, rename it. Nobody dies anymore, they "pass away," they "transition," they "go to a better place." Our loved ones don't leave behind dead bodies, they leave "remains." Funerals are rarely called funerals anymore; they are "celebrations of life," as if grief itself were bad manners. The language is padded, polite, designed not to sting. Even the spaces where we encounter death reflect this strange avoidance. Step into most American funeral homes and you could mistake them for hotel lobbies. The lights are warm and flattering, the air faintly perfumed, the chairs deep enough to swallow you.

Paul Fried

Gentle music hums in the background, carefully chosen so that no note jars the atmosphere. The whole place is designed not for honesty but for comfort.

And what of the bodies themselves? We smooth them, paint them, dress them, rouge their cheeks and comb their hair. The dead are not permitted to look dead. They must look asleep, at peace, untouched. It is called restorative art, but it is really stagecraft. The one moment in life that should pierce us with truth is hidden behind cosmetics.

Meanwhile, outside those hushed rooms, we wage a relentless war against aging. A wrinkle appears, and we rush for creams. A gray hair sprouts, and we book appointments to erase it. Shelves buckle under the weight of products promising to keep us young, serums, powders, supplements, injections. Whole industries thrive on the promise that if we buy enough, inject enough, apply enough, we can stall time. Even Silicon Valley pours fortunes into "longevity labs," billionaires convinced they can out-engineer mortality. And yet no amount of green juice, meditation, or wealth has ever rewritten the one law of existence, all living things eventually die. The oak in your yard, the dog at your feet, your grandmother, you, me.

But because we spend our lives rehearsing distraction, when death finally arrives, we are thrown into chaos. Someone we love takes their last breath and suddenly we are lost in a maze of decisions we have never thought about. We hand the reins to strangers. Doctors with clipboards decide on interventions. Lawyers shuffle papers with legalese none of us can understand in our grief. Funeral directors in dark suits approach us like travel agents selling vacation packages, bronze or mahogany casket, cremation or burial, deluxe or standard service. We nod, sign, and pay, not because it feels right but because we have no script of our own. We've outsourced death because we never learned how to face it.

The cost of that outsourcing is high. When we never learn to look death in the eye, we never learn to live with its shadow. And the shadow is always there. Every birthday candle, every obituary, every empty chair at Thanksgiving is death knocking softly. We hear it, but we pretend not to. Denial becomes our coping mechanism.

Why does the word itself terrify us so? Because death shatters our greatest illusion, control. We build our lives around the idea that we are in charge. We make calendars, track our steps on fitness apps, measure our calories, map out retirement funds, plan five-year goals. We tell ourselves that if we are disciplined enough, careful enough, hard-working enough, we can secure a future. Death mocks that story. It does not wait for mortgages to be paid or for children to finish school. It does not pause for vacation plans or promotions. It arrives without notice, immune to scheduling. It does not care for discipline, wealth, or status. The illusion of control dissolves the moment it appears, and so we pretend we don't hear it.

But denial doesn't save us. It sabotages us. I have seen funerals where death was acknowledged, spoken of openly, where people rose one by one to tell stories, to laugh, to weep. At the funeral of a ninety-seven-year-old Holocaust survivor, I expected perfunctory ritual. Instead, person after person stood to speak. They told of her resilience, her humor, her cooking, her tenderness to strangers. By the end, I felt I knew her intimately. Her story had been honored, her life stitched into memory. Death, in that moment, became not a thief but a teacher.

I have seen the opposite too. I have stood in rooms where funerals were hollow, generic, even careless. Where the officiant mispronounced the name of the deceased. Where siblings muttered angrily at the graveside about who was left out. Where grief was tangled in bitterness because no one knew what the person had wanted. In those moments, silence and avoidance had written the script, and the script was chaos. Families fractured not because someone died, but because no one prepared for what death would mean.

Other cultures handle this differently. In Bhutan, people are taught to contemplate death five times a day, not as morbidity but as gratitude. In Mexico, Día de los Muertos turns grief into a festival of food and memory, a time to invite ancestors back to the table. In many parts of Africa, funerals stretch across days of music and dance, mourning and joy intertwined because death is part of the rhythm of life, not its interruption. The Stoics of Rome carried tokens etched with memento mori, remember you must die, not to wallow in despair but to sharpen their sense of urgency. In medieval Europe, monks kept skulls on their desks as teachers of perspective.

Meanwhile, in America, we whisper. We sanitize. We hide. We turn death into a service to be purchased, not an experience to be integrated. And yet the fear does not lessen, it grows.

Beneath all of this avoidance lies an even deeper fear. We are afraid that death makes life meaningless. If everything ends in silence, in ash, in earth, then what was the point? Why sacrifice? Why risk? Why love fiercely if it all disappears? Death feels like the great eraser. And so we bury the thought.

But here is the paradox, it is precisely because death is inevitable that life has meaning. If we lived forever, nothing would matter.

Days would blur, choices would lose urgency, love would carry no weight. Death is the deadline that makes the project important. It is the final chapter that makes the story worth reading. Without it, there would be no urgency, no savoring, no fire. We fear death makes life meaningless, when in truth it is the very thing that gives life meaning.

And yet, by avoiding death, we rob ourselves of intimacy, preparation, and legacy. Parents do not speak to children about their wishes. Families leave one another to improvise in the dark. Doctors and lawyers and funeral directors end up making decisions for people who never found the courage to speak for themselves. The result is not peace but resentment. Not love but guilt. Not clarity but confusion.

But it does not have to be this way. Imagine a family where the mother sat her children down and said, "Here is what I want, here is where the papers are, here is how to honor me." Imagine a father who wrote his wishes in a letter, or recorded a message, or simply spoke aloud what mattered to him. Those families still grieve. They still ache. But their grief has room to breathe. It is not poisoned by uncertainty. They know what to do, and that knowing is a final gift.

Now imagine the opposite. Families scrambling through file cabinets, fighting in lawyers' offices, bickering over hymns and caskets. Their grief becomes heavier, messier, twisted by resentment. They are not only grieving the person, they are grieving the silence.

Facing death is not about despair. It is about freedom. It is about living more fully because you know time is short. It is about responsibility, because silence is too heavy a burden to leave on the shoulders of those you love.

If you have read this far, you have already done more than most. You have looked death in the eye long enough to keep reading. That alone is an act of courage. Take another step. Write a letter to someone you love, not about your death, but about your life. Tell them what they mean to you. Speak the name of someone who has died at dinner. Invite them back into the room. Ask your parents or your children what they would want if something happened. Sit quietly for five minutes and picture your own funeral, who is there, what is said, what is remembered. Let that vision guide how you live tomorrow.

Because planning for death is not about dying. It is about living, urgently, honestly, responsibly. It is about refusing to hand your silence to the people you love most. It is about leaving behind not confusion but clarity. Not chaos but love.

Chapter

2

THE UNSPOKEN WEIGHT

If Chapter 1 was about how we avoid death, then the next step is facing what that avoidance costs us. Silence is not neutral. We like to pretend it is, that by not talking about wills, or funerals, or advance directives, we've kept life lighter, easier, free from worry. But silence is heavy. It hangs in rooms, presses into families, settles like fog over generations. It creates confusion in the moments when clarity matters most, and it leaves scars that last far longer than a funeral service.

I have seen it at hospital bedsides. A mother drifts in and out of consciousness while her children whisper in the hallway about what she would have wanted. One insists she would want every possible machine, every effort to keep her alive. Another swears she would have wanted comfort only, not a prolonged battle. The spouse sits frozen, too paralyzed by grief to speak. The doctors wait with questions. Decisions must be made. Voices rise, tears spill, and all the while the woman, who once had every chance to share her wishes, lies silent. That is what avoidance does. It doesn't erase hard choices. It multiplies them. It transfers the burden from the one person who could have spoken clearly to the ones least prepared to carry it.

We tell ourselves we'll get around to it someday. I'll write a will when the kids are grown. I'll talk about it when I retire. We'll sit down after the next vacation, after the new job, after things settle down. But here is the truth, life does not settle down. It never does. There is always another distraction, another crisis, another reason to delay. Later becomes the most dangerous word in the English language. Later is a fantasy. Later often disappears without warning. A diagnosis, an accident, a phone call in the middle of the night, and suddenly all the conversations you promised yourself you'd have someday are needed immediately, and it is already too late. I once knew a family whose father prided himself on being organized. He color-coded his files, kept meticulous records of bills and bank accounts, and lectured his children about responsibility. But he never wrote a will. When he died unexpectedly, his estate lingered in probate for more than three years. His children drained their savings accounts to pay lawyers. They sat in courtrooms listening to strangers argue about what their father would have wanted. At one point, two siblings who had spoken every day of their lives stopped speaking altogether. Their relationship shattered not by the death itself, but by the silence that preceded it.

By contrast, I met a woman who left behind a binder. Inside were her medical directives, her funeral preferences, copies of her accounts, even letters for each child. Her family still grieved. They still wept and missed her. But their grief was uncluttered. It had space to breathe. They didn't have to guess. They didn't have to fight. They held each other instead of shoving one another apart. That binder became a final act of love, proof that her care extended beyond her life.

This is the difference between silence and preparation. Silence is not light, it is crushing. Preparation does not add burden, it lifts it. Planning is not cold paperwork, it is emotional architecture. It builds or it breaks.

We resist it because we think it's too early. We tell ourselves we're too young, too healthy, that planning is for later. But planning early isn't about death at all. It's about life. When you make decisions ahead of time, you don't just spare your family confusion someday. You give yourself clarity now. You know your values. You know what kind of legacy you want to leave. That knowledge seeps into the way you live. It shapes your priorities, your choices, your relationships. It is not waiting until the end; it is living the middle more honestly.

The costs of silence are not just financial. Yes, probate fees and legal battles drain resources. Yes, funerals can become expensive mazes. But the true cost is measured in relationships. I have watched siblings fracture over jewelry, brothers fight over tools, cousins split into factions over who gets to "run" the funeral. These conflicts aren't really about necklaces or lawnmowers or hymn choices. They are about absence. They are about children left without clarity, about people left to interpret silence in the raw heat of grief. Money eventually gets sorted. Property eventually gets divided. But bitterness often does not heal.

When families avoid these conversations, the silence becomes its own kind of secret. Everyone knows it's there. Everyone tiptoes around it. Children sense it but don't name it. Spouses avoid it in order to keep the mood "light." It sits in the corner like an elephant, bending every conversation around it. And when the silence is finally broken, it is rarely in a moment of calm. It is broken in a waiting room. Or at the edge of a hospital bed. Or worse, after the funeral, when the questions are no longer about care but about possessions. What did Dad want with the house? What did Mom say about the family photos? Who deserves what? And when no one has the answer, the silence mutates into shouting.

Avoidance is often framed as kindness. Parents say, "I don't want to depress my kids." Spouses say, "I don't want to burden you." But silence is not kindness. It is a burden in disguise. It is confusion wrapped in grief. And grief on its own is already too heavy.

I once spoke to a man whose father died of a heart attack. He told me what stunned him most wasn't the death itself, but the avalanche of decisions that followed. "There I was," he said, "picking out a casket two hours after watching my dad's body get wheeled into the morgue. I didn't know what music he wanted. I didn't know if he wanted burial or cremation. Every choice felt like a test I hadn't studied for, and if I got the answer wrong, I knew it would haunt me." He paused, then said something that has stayed with me ever since, "I would have given anything for just one conversation with him. Just one. But we never had it, because he thought it would be depressing. You know what was depressing? Standing in a funeral home and realizing I didn't actually know my own father's wishes."

This is the inheritance most common in America, not money, not jewelry, but unfinished business. Children inherit guilt, anger, confusion, the heavy sense that they failed a test they never had a chance to prepare for. These inheritances poison families from the inside out. Unlike property, they cannot be sold, split, or donated away. They linger. They fester.

The truth is that planning is not morbid. It is love in one of its hardest, most courageous forms. Writing a will, naming a healthcare proxy, stating your wishes, it says, "I don't want you to carry the weight of my silence." It says, "I want you to grieve without guilt." It says, "I thought of you enough to spare you from chaos." We spend our lives protecting the people we love. We lock doors at night. We teach our kids to look both ways before crossing the street. We buy insurance. Why would that protection stop at the edge of death? The hardest conversations are often the most loving ones.

The story we leave behind is shaped not just by how we lived, but by what we left unfinished. I once spoke to a woman who said, "I loved my mother deeply, but every time I think of her, I remember the fight in the parking lot after her funeral about who was going to pay for what. That memory overshadows the good ones." That broke my heart. Her mother likely spent her life loving her children, but her silence in the end rewrote part of her legacy. Preparation doesn't erase grief, but it protects the story of a life from being rewritten by chaos.

People often tell me they'll plan later because it feels too depressing now. But when you dig into that excuse, you find fear, not practicality. Fear of facing mortality. Fear of conflict. Fear of paperwork. Avoiding those fears doesn't shrink them; it hands them to the people you love. It's like walking out of a burning house and tossing the fire extinguisher back inside to your kids. You think you're sparing yourself, but you're setting them up for chaos.

The irony is that once people finally do the work, they almost always feel lighter. I've watched people sign a will and leave their lawyer's office visibly relieved. "That wasn't nearly as bad as I thought," they say. Or, "I should have done this years ago." Clarity does not add weight; it lifts it. Once the papers are written, the wishes are named, the conversations had, a quiet freedom sneaks in. You can stop worrying about the what-ifs and get back to living.

And here is something people rarely consider, preparation doesn't just protect the next generation. It transforms the present one. Families that talk openly about death also talk more openly about life. Parents share stories they never would have. Children learn about values and priorities. Spouses align not just on paperwork but on meaning. Conversations about end-of-life wishes ripple outward into conversations about how to live now. Honesty in one area creates honesty in others. Suddenly, the silence shrinks. Families who once avoided the topic laugh together about song choices, cry together over memories, hold each other tighter in recognition of life's fragility.

Avoidance feels safe, but it is a trap. Silence feels easy, but it is a burden. The real safety, the real ease, the real love live in preparation. When you prepare, you protect your family from chaos. You give them room to grieve honestly. You give them the chance to celebrate you without being crushed by confusion. You give them, in the end, one more gift, freedom.

Avoiding death does not spare pain. It multiplies it. Facing it does not hasten it. It lightens it. To plan is to love. To stay silent is to leave weight. Which inheritance do you want to leave behind?

Chapter

3

THE FRAGILE ILLUSION OF CONTROL

If there is one myth modern life clings to more tightly than any other, it is the myth of control. We build calendars, track our steps, manage our calories, chart our careers, budget our money, all with the sense that if we just work hard enough, if we just organize carefully enough, if we just keep hustling, we can bend the future to our will. We love control because it feels like safety. It feels like proof that chaos won't swallow us, that we are steering the ship, that the storm might rage but we are at the helm with hands on the wheel. It is comforting to believe that the right combination of discipline and foresight can guarantee the outcome. But death laughs at this myth, because nothing exposes the limits of control faster than mortality.

From the moment we are born, life begins unraveling in directions we cannot script. We think we can chart the course, and in some ways we can, through effort, through choices, through persistence. But always there are forces beyond us, currents stronger than our grip. You can eat kale every day, run marathons, meditate, avoid every vice, and still collapse from a sudden heart attack in your fifties. You can save diligently, plan retirement trips down to the last detail, only to die two months after you stop working. You can be reckless and live to ninety. You can be cautious and go at thirty. Death does not calculate based on our careful preparations. It comes when it comes.

The illusion of control seduces us into believing we are exempt. We watch tragedies on the news and say, "That won't be me. That happens to other people, not to us." We comfort ourselves with statistics, averages, probabilities, as though percentages could grant us immunity. But the truth is brutal in its simplicity, every single person dies. We know it, but we behave as though we might be the exception. That's the trick denial plays, we acknowledge death abstractly but not personally. Death is real in general but unreal in particular.

This illusion is not new. Humans have always tried to bargain with fate. Ancient kings built monuments to themselves, convinced their legacies would make them immortal. Pharaohs stuffed tombs with treasures to carry into the next world, as though wealth could buy eternity. Alchemists spent lifetimes searching for elixirs. Explorers sought fountains of youth. Today's billionaires fund biotech labs and upload their memories into hard drives. The costumes change, but the play is the same. We want control over the one reality that refuses to bow to us.

But control is fragile. It shatters the moment illness enters the room. Ask anyone who has sat across from a doctor as the words "stage four" fell into the air. In that moment, every calendar, every plan, every illusion dissolves. Control was never real, only rented. Or ask the spouse who answers the phone at 2 a.m. to learn of a car accident. Ask the parent who watches a child's life support machine shut down. In those moments, the myth is exposed. Life was never under our command.

Live Fully. Leave Wisely.

The irony is that when we believe most strongly in our control, we are most easily undone. People who cling tightly to the idea that they can manage everything are often the ones who struggle the most when control slips through their fingers. They resist, deny, rage, panic. They fight to maintain the illusion long after it has crumbled. Meanwhile, those who have learned to accept uncertainty, who have made peace with the limits of control, who know that chaos is part of the bargain, are often steadier. They may grieve, but they do not collapse under the weight of disillusionment.

I once knew a man who was the very definition of control. He ran a business with military precision, his days segmented into color-coded blocks, his finances balanced down to the penny. He prided himself on never being caught off guard. But when he was diagnosed with aggressive cancer, his world unraveled. Every day he asked, "How could this happen? I did everything right." His final months were filled not just with physical pain but with a deep bitterness, as though death were cheating him out of a contract he believed he had signed. Contrast that with a woman I met who, upon learning of her terminal illness, told her children, "We don't get to choose how long the story is. We only get to choose how we live the chapters we're given." She laughed often in those final months, gave away possessions joyfully, told stories, recorded messages for her grandchildren. Both faced the same ending, but one shattered under the illusion of control, while the other found freedom in surrender.

We confuse control with certainty, but they are not the same. Certainty is impossible; control is fragile. What we actually need is clarity. Clarity is not about bending the future to our will, but about naming what matters to us most so that when uncertainty arrives, and it always will, we are not lost. A will, an advance directive, a legacy plan, these are not instruments of control, they are instruments of clarity. They don't change the inevitability of death, but they change the experience of it. They turn chaos into guidance. They transform silence into voice.

This is where the illusion of control is so dangerous. Because while we are busy pretending we are steering everything, we fail to do the one thing actually within our power, prepare. We spend endless energy trying to outsmart aging, but almost none making sure our children know our wishes. We pour money into vitamins and creams, but not into clarity. We track calories but not beneficiaries. We plan vacations in detail but leave our deaths unspoken. It is the ultimate misalignment of priorities, born from the myth that if we just keep pretending, maybe we'll avoid the inevitable.

Our culture reinforces this illusion at every turn. Advertisements promise "forever young." Self-help books assure us we can manifest anything. Social media shows highlight reels, carefully curated to suggest that if we just optimize, if we just hustle, if we just buy the right product, we can control our destinies. The market thrives on our denial. If we all accepted our mortality tomorrow, half of the wellness industry would collapse overnight. The denial of death is profitable.

But there are cracks in the facade. Look closer and you'll see it. You'll see it in the quiet panic of people approaching retirement who realize time is not infinite. You'll see it in the desperation of patients seeking one more experimental treatment even when the prognosis is hopeless. You'll see it in the endless ways we distract ourselves, streaming, scrolling, consuming, anything to drown out the tick of the clock. Beneath all of it is fear, not just fear of death itself, but fear of the loss of control.

And yet, those who have learned to face death differently tell another story. They are not free from fear, but they are not paralyzed by it. They do not mistake preparation for morbidity; they see it as liberation. They know that the real freedom comes not from pretending we can control everything, but from naming what matters when control inevitably slips away. I have heard people describe the relief they feel after finishing a will or completing an advance directive. "It feels like a weight lifted," they say. "I didn't realize how much it was nagging at me." In truth, the illusion of control is heavy, because deep down we know it's a lie. Preparation replaces illusion with clarity, and clarity is light.

The fragile illusion of control not only distorts our view of death, it distorts our view of life. When we believe we are in charge of everything, we become rigid. We chase perfection, avoid risk, delay joy until the "right time." But death reminds us there may never be a "right time." The trip we postpone might never happen. The words we plan to say someday might never be heard. The embrace we keep meaning to give might never be felt. Death shatters control, but in doing so it gives us urgency. It forces us to live now, not later.

There is a strange freedom in surrendering the illusion. When we stop pretending we can control everything, we begin to notice the things that actually matter. We notice the laughter of our children, the warmth of a hand held in silence, the taste of a meal savored slowly, the beauty of an ordinary day. We forgive faster. We argue less about trivialities. We invest more deeply in love and less in appearances. Death, ironically, becomes not an enemy but a tutor.

So the question is not whether we can control life. We cannot. The question is whether we will continue clinging to the illusion until it breaks us, or whether we will embrace clarity instead. Clarity that says, I cannot stop the storm, but I can leave instructions for the ones who must sail through it. Clarity that says, I cannot decide when my story ends, but I can decide how my story is remembered. Clarity that says, I cannot promise immortality, but I can leave love instead of chaos.

The illusion of control is seductive, but it is brittle. The moment life cracks it open, we are left scrambling. Letting go of that illusion is not weakness, it is courage. It is choosing to live honestly rather than pretending. It is choosing to prepare rather than to burden. It is choosing to love in the hardest and most lasting way, by acknowledging the truth and acting on it.

In the end, control is a mirage. Clarity is real. And when death finally arrives, and it always will, clarity is the one gift we can still give.

Chapter

4

WHEN SILENCE HURTS

There are few moments in life more haunting than the silence that follows death. Not the silence of a room after mourners leave, not the quiet of a cemetery, but the silence of unanswered questions. The silence of not knowing what someone would have wanted. The silence of paperwork left undone, conversations left unspoken, decisions left to be guessed at in the worst possible moment. This silence is not peace. It is weight. It is confusion disguised as calm, a burden that lingers long after the funeral flowers have wilted.

I have seen that silence take shape in hospital waiting rooms, where families gather under fluorescent lights, their faces pale from sleeplessness, their bodies folded into uncomfortable chairs. The air is heavy with grief and indecision. A son insists his mother would want every possible intervention, every machine, every chance. A daughter argues that she would not want to be kept alive in that way, that her dignity mattered more. A spouse sits paralyzed, afraid to make a choice that feels like betrayal. The doctors wait, needing answers. And no one in that room is wrong. Each is trying, in their own way, to love. But without guidance, love turns into conflict. What should be a moment of solidarity becomes a battlefield of interpretation. And long after the machines are turned off, the scars of that silence remain.

I once spoke to a man who carried such a scar for decades. His father suffered a massive stroke and never regained consciousness. The family argued for weeks. Some wanted to continue treatment. Others wanted to let him go. No one knew what he would have wanted. When the decision finally came, it left his son haunted. Years later, he told me he still woke at night wondering if he had "pulled the plug too early." His words were heavy, his eyes clouded. Time had not healed the doubt. Silence had planted it, and it grew like a weed that would not die.

Silence does not only haunt the living in medical decisions. It follows families into the practical matters of death too. The unspoken wishes about funerals, the absence of a will, the lack of instructions. I have sat with siblings who fought over a mother's jewelry not because they cared about the objects themselves but because the objects became symbols of who was loved most, of who deserved more. I have listened to cousins argue over whether a father wanted burial or cremation, each convinced their memory was truer. I have seen families fracture over furniture, photographs, even kitchen utensils. And when you look closely, you see the truth, these fights were never really about things. They were about silence. They were about children left to fill in blanks that could have been filled by one simple conversation.

We think we are sparing our families by staying silent. We tell ourselves we don't want to depress them, don't want to burden them with morbid details, don't want to take away the lightness of everyday life. We tell ourselves there will be time later. Later, when the kids are grown. Later, when we retire. Later, when life slows down. But later has a way of evaporating. Later often

Live Fully. Leave Wisely.

never arrives. Silence that was meant to protect becomes the very thing that wounds.

Silence also carries unspoken rules. In many families, it is not just death that is avoided but the conversations around it. Children grow up knowing they are not supposed to ask. Spouses learn to change the subject when the word comes up. Whole households operate with an unspoken agreement, we do not talk about this. And yet everyone feels the weight of what is missing. It hangs in the background, unacknowledged but powerful, shaping decisions through its absence.

There is another form of silence that hurts, and it is the silence of regret. I knew a woman whose father died suddenly in his sixties. She told me she could not remember the last words she said to him. They had argued weeks earlier, and she assumed there would be time to reconcile. His death stole that chance, and the silence between them became unbearable. She carried it like a stone in her chest. "If I had just one more day," she said, "I would fill it with everything I never said." That is another weight silence leaves us wit, the words we withhold, the love we postpone, the forgiveness we never give because we assume tomorrow will be available.

Some silences are cultural. In America, death is treated as impolite dinner conversation. We are quick to share medical updates, job changes, gossip, but death we whisper about, if we mention it at all. In some families, this silence comes from fear. In others, from superstition, the belief that naming it might invite it closer. But avoidance does not keep it away. It only ensures that when it comes, we are unready.

Other cultures do not make the same mistake. In Mexico, Día de los Muertos invites the dead back into conversation. In parts of Africa, funerals are community affairs lasting days, with laughter, song, and storytelling. In Bhutan, people are taught to contemplate death daily, not as morbidity but as gratitude. These cultures know that silence is not protection. Speaking of death does not hasten it. It only prepares us to meet it with honesty.

The silence around death in America creates an inheritance most of us don't think about. Not money or property, but unfinished business. Children inherit guilt. Spouses inherit doubt. Friends inherit confusion. Silence is passed down like an heirloom, and it weighs more than any casket.

Yet there is a paradox here. For as much as we fear breaking the silence, the act itself often brings relief. I have seen families finally gather to talk openly about end-of-life wishes, and the tension breaks like a storm giving way to clear air. Tears come, but so does laughter. Memories flow. Children who had tiptoed around the subject for years feel closer to their parents, not further. What seemed unbearable to speak becomes unbearable not to speak. And afterward, everyone feels lighter. The weight that hovered over them shrinks the moment it is named.

I remember a man who told me he and his father had finally discussed funeral plans. "It was awkward for five minutes," he admitted. "But then he told me what songs he wanted, and we ended up laughing about his terrible taste in music. Now, when the time comes, I'll know what to do. And I'll smile when I hear those songs, because I'll know we talked about it together." The silence that once loomed between them dissolved into intimacy. That is the strange gift of honesty, it replaces fear with closeness.

The truth is, silence hurts most when it arrives in moments of crisis. Hospitals, funeral homes, probate court, these are not places to guess at what a loved one wanted. These are not moments when our minds and hearts are clear. They are moments when we are shaken, when grief clouds judgment, when emotions overflow. To leave decisions until then is to hand the people you love the hardest test of their lives without a single note of preparation.

It is easy to imagine that silence keeps us safe. It delays the discomfort of a difficult conversation. It allows us to continue pretending life will go on forever. But silence is a debt, and debts always come due. The payment is confusion, conflict, guilt, resentment. It is siblings who no longer speak. It is children haunted by questions. It is spouses carrying anger into their own deaths.

What breaks silence is courage. And courage in this case does not look like grand gestures. It looks like sitting down at a kitchen table and saying, "Let's talk about this." It looks like writing down wishes, even imperfectly, so that others are not left to guess. It looks like telling your family where the documents are, what matters to you, how you hope to be remembered. It looks like speaking words of love now, instead of waiting until silence makes them impossible.

When silence is broken, it does not erase grief, but it transforms it. Grief with clarity can be honest. It can be shared. It can be about love instead of guilt. Grief with silence becomes confusion. It divides instead of unites. It lingers instead of heals.

We all carry silence, whether we admit it or not. We carry the things we haven't said, the plans we haven't made, the questions we haven't asked. The only choice is whether we will leave that silence as our legacy or whether we will find the courage to replace it with clarity. To stay silent is to wound the people we love most. To speak is to give them one last gift, peace.

Chapter

5

THE STORIES WE LEAVE BEHIND

When death comes, the material things we leave behind often take center stage. Wills are read, possessions are divided, houses are sold, and accounts are closed. Yet when you listen to the conversations that continue years later, when you sit at family gatherings long after the estate has been settled, you realize that the true inheritance we leave behind is not money or property but stories. The way people speak of us, the memories they share, the lessons they pass on to their children, these become the threads that weave our lives into the fabric of the future.

Stories are powerful because they endure in ways that objects cannot. A chair can break, a ring can be lost, money can be spent. But the story of who you were, what you loved, how you treated others, that story continues to ripple forward. Sometimes it is told in words, sometimes in actions, sometimes in quiet rituals that nobody even realizes began with you. A granddaughter may stir soup the way her grandmother once did, humming a tune she cannot quite place. A son may pause at a crossroads and hear his father's advice in his own mind. A neighbor may remember the way you always waved from the porch and find themselves doing the same.

The stories we leave behind can be blessings or burdens. They can inspire or they can wound. Some stories are carried with warmth and pride, repeated with laughter and love. Others are carried like scars, whispered in bitterness or sadness. The difference lies in how we lived and how we prepared. A life of connection and courage leaves stories that nourish. A life of silence and avoidance leaves stories that weigh.

I once met a woman who carried a story of her father that was as heavy as it was invisible. He was a man of few words, successful in his career but emotionally distant at home. He never told her he was proud of her. He never said I love you. When he died, he left behind money and a well-ordered estate, but no words, no letters, no guidance. His silence became the story she carried. Decades later, she still longed for a sentence that never came. His legacy was not his wealth, but the absence of affirmation. She told me she would have given up every dollar for one conversation where he spoke his heart.

Contrast that with another story I witnessed. A mother of three had spent years writing small letters to each of her children. She tucked them into drawers, slipped them into books, left them in boxes marked for the future. When she passed away, her children discovered a treasure trove of notes. Some were short and playful, some were long and reflective, but all carried her voice, her humor, her love. Her children said they felt like she was still speaking to them. Her story became not absence but presence. They carried her words forward with joy, sharing them with grandchildren who would never meet her in person.

The difference between these two stories was not luck. It was choice. One parent chose silence, the other chose to speak. Both left behind legacies, but only one left behind a legacy of clarity and love.

Our culture often confuses legacy with inheritance. We think of it in terms of what we own rather than who we are. We assume that the primary story will be written by the objects we pass down. Yet objects are only vessels. It is the meaning attached to them that endures. A wedding ring is just a circle of metal until it is remembered as the ring worn by a grandmother who stayed married for fifty years through hardship and joy. A recipe card is just ink on paper until it becomes the reminder of holiday dinners filled with laughter. A photograph is just a piece of paper until it becomes the image of a father smiling, capturing the way he looked when he was happiest.

The danger of leaving our story unspoken is that others will write it for us. When wishes are not expressed, when values are not named, when words are not spoken, silence fills the gaps. And silence often distorts. Children may assume you did not care. Spouses may believe you avoided the truth out of selfishness. Friends may wonder if your distance was intentional. Stories created by silence are rarely kind. They are shaped by grief, confusion, and doubt.

Every life leaves behind an inheritance of story. The only question is what kind of story it will be. Will it be a story of preparation, of thoughtfulness, of love expressed clearly? Or will it be a story of confusion, of fights over possessions, of regrets that never fade? The choice is ours, but the consequences are theirs.

Live Fully. Leave Wisely.

I remember a family who discovered after their father's death that he had left no will. He had been a meticulous man in life, but he always said he would "get around to it later." Later never came. His children spent years in probate court, draining money and energy while arguing over decisions he could have made in a single afternoon. The story they told afterward was not of his kindness or his hard work. It was of the chaos he left them. It became the defining story of his death, overshadowing the stories of his life.

And then there was a friend whose mother left not only a will but also a binder filled with notes. She had outlined her medical wishes, her funeral preferences, even songs she wanted played. She had written each of her children letters of love and apology, forgiving old wounds, affirming her pride. At her funeral, instead of bitterness, there was peace. Her children spoke of her foresight as one of her greatest gifts. The story they told was of her love, not her silence.

The stories we leave are not always deliberate. Sometimes they are born of habits. A father who is always late leaves a story of absence. A mother who always listens leaves a story of presence. A friend who always remembers birthdays leaves a story of thoughtfulness. These stories accumulate quietly until they become the defining memories of a person's life.

The risk of ignoring this truth is that we leave behind unintended stories. Neglect becomes a story. Avoidance becomes a story. Silence becomes a story. Even cruelty, if not healed or acknowledged, becomes a story. And those stories ripple forward through generations. A child who never heard "I love you" may struggle to say it to their own children. A family torn apart by unspoken decisions may repeat the same silence in the next generation. The story multiplies.

Yet just as silence multiplies, so does courage. A parent who chooses to speak honestly about death teaches their children not to fear it. A grandparent who writes down family traditions teaches grandchildren to carry them forward. A spouse who shares openly about wishes for the future models vulnerability and trust. These choices create stories of love, and those stories ripple forward too.

There is a man I know whose grandfather survived the Holocaust. He lost nearly everything, but he carried forward one simple practice. Every night, no matter what, the family ate dinner together. No excuses, no interruptions, no silence at the table. That practice became a sacred tradition. Decades later, long after the grandfather's death, the family still gathers for nightly dinners. His story of survival and connection became their story too. One man's choice echoed into generations he never met.

This is the truth of legacy. It is not optional. We cannot decide whether or not we will leave a story. We can only decide what kind of story it will be. And the difference often comes down to preparation.

When we prepare, we write our own story. We decide how we will be remembered. We give clarity instead of confusion. We offer guidance instead of silence. We replace guilt with gratitude. When we avoid, we let the story be written by chance, by grief, by conflict. And chance is rarely kind.

The stories we leave behind also shape how our loved ones grieve. Grief without clarity is heavier, tangled with questions and regrets. Grief with clarity, while still painful, allows for love to shine through. When someone knows exactly what their parent wanted, they can grieve without guilt. They can focus on remembering, not second-guessing. They can tell stories of love instead of stories of doubt.

The most powerful stories are not the ones told at funerals by officiants who barely knew the person. They are the ones told at kitchen tables years later. They are the ones whispered to grandchildren. They are the ones that become rituals, traditions, habits. They are the quiet inheritance that money cannot match.

So the question is not whether you will leave a story. You already are, every day. The question is whether it will be a story of silence or a story of love. A story of avoidance or a story of courage. A story of chaos or a story of peace.

It is easier than we imagine to begin shaping that story. It starts with speaking words that too often go unsaid. Telling your children you are proud of them. Writing a letter to a spouse. Recording a memory. Choosing a song. Making a plan. These acts may feel small, but they accumulate. Over time, they become the framework of a story that will endure long after you are gone.

Because one day, someone will sit at a table and speak your name. They will tell a story of you. And the story they tell will not come from the objects you left but from the love you gave, the clarity you offered, the courage you showed. That story is your true inheritance. That story is your legacy.

Chapter

6

HEALTH CARE DECISIONS

If a will speaks after you are gone, an advance directive speaks when you cannot. Few decisions carry more weight than those made in a hospital room when a loved one lies silent, unable to speak for themselves. Families often gather around a bed with faces drawn from sleepless nights and hearts torn in different directions. Some insist on doing everything possible to prolong life, clinging to machines and treatments as though they are ropes holding someone from falling. Others whisper that comfort is more important, that suffering should not be stretched out for the sake of more days. The doctors stand waiting for instructions, the machines hum, and the silence becomes unbearable.

I have seen families fractured in those moments. A husband frozen, unable to make a choice, children arguing in voices so sharp they echo in the sterile hallways, nurses hovering with quiet patience while decisions hang in the air. No one in the room is wrong, but without guidance, every choice feels wrong. And long after the machines have been turned off, or left on, long after the monitors fall silent, the arguments do not end.

Live Fully. Leave Wisely.

They echo in the memories of those who lived them, shaping how grief unfolds. Years later, a son may wonder if he acted too soon, while a daughter may still believe they did not do enough.

That is the cruel weight of silence. When a person does not leave clear instructions, when they do not share their values and wishes, the people they love most are left to guess. And guessing is not love's best gift. Guessing leaves behind scars.

An advance directive, sometimes called a living will, is the tool that can take away that burden. It is not complicated, though many imagine it to be. It is a document where you decide how you wish to be treated when you cannot speak for yourself. It covers questions of life support, ventilators, feeding tubes, resuscitation, organ donation, pain management, and even the setting where you would prefer to spend your last days. But perhaps the most important part is naming a healthcare proxy, someone you trust to be your voice. This is not a stranger, not a lawyer, not a doctor. It is the person you believe will honor your values when you cannot explain them.

The importance of this cannot be overstated. Without it, decisions are left to those least prepared to make them. Imagine a spouse sitting in a waiting room with doctors pressing for answers and children shouting over what they believe is right. Imagine the guilt that attaches itself to every decision made in confusion. Now imagine the same room with a folder in hand, the voice of the loved one written down in black and white. The difference is the difference between chaos and clarity, between guilt and gratitude.

I knew a woman whose father had a massive stroke. He never regained consciousness, and for weeks the family debated. One sibling fought for every possible intervention, convinced that to do anything less was betrayal. Another begged to stop treatment, saying their father had always valued quality of life over length. The father had never spoken of it, never written it down, and so the decision became a battlefield. The siblings stopped speaking to each other even after the funeral. The silence of their father became the wound that outlived him.

And then there was another family, one who had heard their mother say it many times. She told them, half joking but with real conviction, that if she could not dance, sing, or hug her grandchildren, she wanted to go in peace. She wrote it down too, in a simple statement that became her advance directive. When the day came, her children gathered and wept, but they did not argue. They knew what she wanted. They honored her wishes. Their grief was real, but it was free of the bitter poison of doubt.

The difference between those two families was not chance. It was preparation. It was one parent choosing to speak while the other remained silent.

We often treat these documents as if they are about medicine, but in truth, they are about dignity. Dignity in how we live our final days. Dignity in where we spend them. Dignity in choosing what fighting for life really means to us. For some, dignity is found in exhausting every possible treatment, demanding that machines breathe when lungs cannot, demanding that surgeons cut and stitch and repair until there is nothing left to try. For others, dignity is found in peace, in comfort, in being at home with family and familiar surroundings rather than fluorescent lights and hospital beds. Neither answer is wrong. What is wrong is not deciding.

The fear that keeps people from making these choices is not fear of paperwork. It is fear of facing mortality. We tell ourselves it is too early, that we are too young, that we will get to it later. We convince ourselves that life will give us time to prepare, that we can wait until after the next vacation, after retirement, after things calm down. But life does not calm down. Illnesses arrive uninvited. Accidents come without warning. Death does not send a calendar invite. Later often turns into never.

I once heard a story of a man who had always promised to put things in writing. He was healthy, active, and saw no reason to rush. Then he collapsed in his kitchen from an aneurysm and never regained consciousness. His wife, bewildered and terrified, had to make every decision alone. She spent years replaying those choices, wondering if she had betrayed him, wondering if he would have wanted more time or less suffering. She loved him deeply, but his silence left her with a burden that never lifted.

Contrast that with a man I met who had been diagnosed with terminal cancer. He sat with his children one evening and laid it out clearly. He wanted no machines, no feeding tubes, no aggressive treatments once quality of life was gone. He wanted music, comfort, and family. He signed his documents and kept them visible in the house. When the time came, his children were sad, but they were not conflicted. They honored him with peace. Years later, they still speak of the grace of those final days, of how his clarity gave them space to grieve without guilt.

Creating an advance directive is not complicated. In most states, it requires nothing more than filling out a form, signing it, and making sure loved ones know where it is. No lawyer is necessary. No large expense is required. And unlike a will that distributes possessions after death, an advance directive is a living document. It can be changed at any time as life changes. Marriage, divorce, new diagnoses, shifts in values, all of these can be reflected with new words and new clarity. The point is not to carve something in stone but to give voice to what matters most right now.

The irony is that once people do it, they often describe feeling lighter. They say it was easier than expected. They say they should have done it years ago. That is because clarity does not add weight, it takes it away. It lifts the fog of uncertainty. It frees families from guessing. It allows love to be expressed in decisions instead of arguments.

There is a strange relief that comes when these conversations are had. They may begin with awkwardness, with people shifting in chairs, with nervous laughter. But once the words are spoken, a new space opens. Families often find themselves sharing more, not less. They speak about fears, about values, about memories. They discover each other in ways they had not before. Talking about death makes room for talking about life.

We spend our lives protecting those we love. We lock the doors at night, wear seatbelts, buy insurance, teach our children to look both ways before crossing the street. Yet many people stop that protection at the edge of death. They leave their families unprepared for the decisions that matter most. Writing down your wishes is not morbid. It is one of the deepest expressions of love. It says, I thought of you. I did not leave this to chance. I cared enough to guide you even when I could not speak.

The greatest gift we can give our families is not the absence of grief. Grief will come no matter what. The gift is the absence of confusion. It is the clarity that allows them to cry without fighting, to mourn without guilt, to gather around a bed or a grave with peace in their hearts rather than bitterness in their voices.

The silence of unspoken wishes is heavy, but the clarity of spoken ones is light. It does not erase sorrow, but it makes sorrow bearable. It does not erase loss, but it makes loss clean instead of tangled. It does not erase death, but it allows love to speak in the hardest moments.

If a will is about possessions, an advance directive is about spirit. Both are important, but one tells the story of what you owned, and the other tells the story of who you were. To leave one without the other is to leave the story unfinished. To prepare both is to leave behind a legacy not just of things but of values.

When we think about what we want our families to remember, it is rarely the material things. It is the moments, the laughter, the traditions, the lessons. By leaving clear healthcare wishes, we ensure that even our final chapter reflects those values. We ensure that our families remember us not for the chaos of indecision, but for the clarity of love.

The truth is that silence in the most critical moments is not love. Love speaks. Love guides. Love prepares. And when our own voices fail, love can live on in the words we left behind.

Chapter

7

BEYOND LEGALITIES

When most people think about planning for the end of life, they think of documents. They picture a will tucked away in a lawyer's office, an advance directive stored in a folder, a life insurance policy filed with the rest of the bills. These things matter, of course. They shape what happens to our belongings, they guide medical decisions, they protect against confusion. But when the last chapter of a life is written, it is rarely the paperwork that people remember. The law can divide possessions, but it cannot mend a broken relationship. It can distribute property, but it cannot distribute forgiveness. It can allocate assets, but it cannot allocate love.

There is a realm that lies beyond the legalities, a realm of story and spirit, of conversations and rituals, of choices made not in courtrooms but in living rooms. To prepare for death fully, one must think not only about who will inherit the house or the bank account, but also about who will inherit the stories, the lessons, and the bonds that made life worth living. These are not the things that lawyers draft, but they are the things that endure far longer than any contract.

Live Fully. Leave Wisely.

I once knew a man who prided himself on his precision. His will was impeccable, his estate meticulously planned. He had binders with tabs, instructions for every account, passwords written and updated. But he had never spoken openly to his children about his values, his regrets, or his dreams for them. When he died, the settlement of his estate was smooth and quick, but his children felt oddly empty. They had inherited wealth, but not meaning. They had clarity on assets, but not on their father. They were left with a legal legacy, but not an emotional one.

Contrast that with a woman whose financial situation was modest. She had little to leave in the way of possessions, but she had left behind boxes of letters, recordings of family stories, recipes written in her own hand, and a clear description of the traditions she hoped would continue. Her children described her passing not as the end of her life but as the beginning of a story they could carry forward. They did not inherit wealth, but they inherited richness. Every holiday, they cooked her meals. Every birthday, they shared her stories. Her legacy was not written by law, but by love.

What we often forget is that the law only governs what can be measured. It can measure property, money, and titles. It cannot measure affection, trust, or belonging. Those things live beyond the reach of courts, and yet they are often the very things that families fight over most bitterly. A necklace may be inexpensive, but if it carries the memory of a mother's embrace, it can cause arguments that no lawyer anticipated. A handwritten note may have no material value, but to the child who longs for connection, it is priceless.

Beyond legalities lies the world of meaning. This is the world where silence can be as harmful as a missing will, where unresolved conflicts can fracture families as much as contested estates. It is the world where saying I forgive you matters more than who inherits the car, where saying I love you matters more than who receives the watch. Without these words, no amount of paperwork can create peace. With these words, even the most modest estate can become a source of grace.

Many cultures have long understood this. Rituals often exist not to divide property but to bind people together. In some traditions, families gather after death not only to grieve but to share stories, to sing songs, to repeat the values of the one who has passed. In those moments, the true inheritance becomes visible. It is not in the possessions distributed, but in the bonds strengthened. The law may settle accounts, but ritual and memory settle hearts.

In modern Western culture, we often overlook this. We treat preparation as a legal chore, something to check off a list, an unpleasant but necessary errand. We may sign the papers, but we do not speak the words. We may designate an heir, but we do not designate a blessing. We may organize accounts, but we do not organize memories. The result is that families are left with technical clarity but emotional confusion. They know what to do with the bank accounts, but they do not know what to do with their grief.

The work of preparing beyond legalities is not about forms. It is about courage. It is the courage to speak truths that may be uncomfortable. It is the courage to apologize for past mistakes. It is the courage to forgive others for theirs. It is the courage to say the words that pride or fear has kept locked away. Those words may be awkward, but they can heal wounds that no amount of money can touch.

I recall a story of two brothers who had not spoken for years. Their father had died, leaving behind a carefully drafted will. The property was divided fairly, the finances distributed evenly. Yet at the funeral, the brothers stood on opposite sides of the room, unwilling to look at each other. What their father had not left was reconciliation. He had never insisted they face their estrangement, never spoken the words that might have urged them to mend it. His paperwork was perfect, but his silence was devastating.

On the other hand, I once met a family whose matriarch, knowing her time was short, called her children together. She told them directly that she wanted them united, that no possession mattered more than their bond. She apologized for moments when she had failed them. She blessed each of them with words of love. When she died, her estate was modest, but her family was strong. They told me later that her words carried more weight than any inheritance could have.

This is what it means to prepare beyond legalities. It means asking not only what happens to things, but what happens to people. It means realizing that the story people will tell of you will not be about the distribution of your assets, but about the distribution of your heart. Did you leave them clarity, or did you leave them confusion? Did you leave them love, or did you leave them silence?

In the years that follow a death, people rarely recall the details of the legal process. They recall the conversations. They recall the stories. They recall the way they felt. A daughter may not remember how much money she inherited, but she will remember if her father ever told her he was proud of her. A son may not remember the exact value of a house, but he will remember if his mother ever said she forgave him. These are the inheritances that live on.

To prepare fully, we must engage both realms. The legal documents are necessary, but they are not sufficient. They create order, but they do not create meaning. The human work must be done alongside them. That work may be harder, because it asks us to look inward, to admit our regrets, to express our love. Yet that work is the truest gift we can give.

The law will handle your estate. But only you can handle your story. Only you can decide to leave behind not just possessions but peace. Only you can choose to speak the words that will echo long after the lawyers have finished their work.

When we think about legacy, we must ask ourselves not only who will inherit our things, but who will inherit our presence. Who will carry our laughter. Who will pass down our recipes. Who will remember our songs. Who will teach our lessons. These are the inheritances that cannot be drafted in contracts, but they are the ones that shape generations.

In the end, preparing beyond legalities is about seeing clearly what truly matters. Money can support, but it cannot heal. Property can shelter, but it cannot comfort. The law can settle accounts, but it cannot settle hearts. That work is ours to do while we still have time. It requires no lawyer, only honesty. It requires no courtroom, only a conversation. It requires no signature, only the courage to speak.

Because when our time comes, and it will, our families will sit together and remember. They will speak our names. They will tell stories. They will laugh, they will weep, they will argue, they will reconcile. And the story they tell will not be about how carefully the paperwork was written. It will be about how carefully the life was lived. It will be about what we left them, not in bank accounts, but in hearts.

Beyond legalities lies the realm of love. It is the realm where legacies are not measured in dollars but in memories. It is the realm where the true inheritance is not property but presence. It is the realm where silence is the heaviest burden and words are the greatest gift. To prepare fully, we must step into that realm with courage, and we must do it while we still can.

Chapter

8

GRIEF AS LOVE

When someone we love dies, the world shifts. The phone call comes, the words are spoken, the breath leaves the body, and suddenly life as we knew it collapses. We call it grief, and we treat it as something unwelcome, something to endure, something to push through until we are whole again. But grief is not a mistake in the design of life. It is not an illness that needs to be cured or a weakness that needs to be hidden. Grief is love, transformed by absence. It is the proof that a bond existed so deeply that its breaking leaves us changed forever.

We often misunderstand grief in modern culture. We are taught to be efficient and forward-moving, to keep pace with work and obligations, to measure healing in days or weeks as though the heart can be managed by a calendar. People say things like time heals all wounds or you will move on or at least they lived a long life. They offer these words like bandages, hoping to cover what feels too raw to touch. But grief does not obey timelines. It does not follow rules. It does not lessen because a person was old or because the relationship was complicated. It lingers, it bends, it returns. It comes not only in tears but also in silence, in laughter, in sudden waves that crash when you least expect them.

I once sat with a widower who told me the hardest part of his loss was not the night his wife died but the months afterward. At the funeral, everyone was there. Friends brought food, neighbors filled the house, cards arrived in the mail. But six months later, the house was quiet. Everyone else had gone back to their lives. He still woke up to an empty bed, still reached across in the night to find her side cold, still turned to share a thought and found only silence. What he longed for was not for grief to end, but for someone to understand that it had not ended. For him, grief was not just the memory of his wife's death, it was the daily reminder of their love.

That is the heart of grief. It is not an enemy of love but its twin. We grieve only because we loved. The depth of our grief measures the depth of our bond. When someone says you should be over it by now, what they fail to understand is that what they are asking is for you to love less. To diminish grief would be to diminish love. And no one who has truly loved wishes for that.

Our society has not given grief the place it deserves. In other times and places, mourning was honored with rituals. Black clothes were worn for months or years. Communities gathered for long periods of remembrance. Songs were sung, prayers repeated, stories told over and over until they became woven into the fabric of life. Grief was not rushed. It was witnessed. Today, we have shortened those rituals. We offer three days off work, sometimes a week, and then we expect people to return as if nothing has changed. We have lost the patience to sit with sorrow, and in doing so, we have left the grieving to carry their love alone.

Yet grief, when embraced, is not only a burden. It is also a teacher. It teaches us about the fragility of life. It teaches us about the power of memory. It teaches us about what really matters. Those who have grieved often live differently. They laugh more freely, knowing laughter is precious. They forgive faster, knowing time is short. They cherish small moments, because they understand that ordinary days are the real treasures of life.

I remember a daughter who told me about her mother's death. She said, I thought the world would end when she died. Instead, it kept turning, but I saw it differently. Every sunrise reminded me of her. Every meal I cooked felt like a conversation with her. I grieved, but I also lived more awake than I ever had before. Grief turned into a way of seeing, a way of noticing. It did not erase my mother, it kept her alive in me.

This is what it means to understand grief as love. It is not something to get past but something to carry. At first, the carrying feels unbearable. The weight crushes you, steals your breath, leaves you gasping. But over time, you do not get rid of the weight. Instead, you grow stronger. You learn to carry it differently. It becomes part of you, shaping the way you live, the way you love, the way you remember. The stone remains, but you are no longer crushed beneath it.

Too often, those who grieve are told to find closure, as if grief were a door that could be shut or a wound that could be stitched clean. But closure is not what love asks for. Love asks to be remembered, honored, carried forward. The goal is not to close grief, but to weave it into life. To let it remind us that someone mattered, that someone still matters, that someone loved us enough to leave an ache in their absence.

Communities play a role here too. Grief is not meant to be carried in isolation. When neighbors bring food, when friends tell stories, when someone simply sits in silence beside us, grief becomes bearable. The burden does not lessen, but the shoulders that carry it multiply. I have seen neighborhoods rally around widows, gathering every week for dinner for months, even years. I have seen churches create spaces where names are spoken aloud again and again so the dead are never forgotten. These are not small gestures. They are lifelines. They remind the grieving that love is not gone, it has simply changed form.

There is danger in avoiding grief. When grief is hidden, it festers. It turns into anger, resentment, numbness. It isolates. People stop talking about the one who died for fear of causing pain, but silence wounds more than words. Speaking the name, telling the story, remembering the laugh, these things do not deepen the wound. They heal it. They remind us that love is still alive, even if the person is not.

Grief is not linear. It does not move neatly from denial to anger to acceptance as diagrams suggest. It circles back on itself, rises and falls like waves. One day you may laugh, the next you may collapse in tears. Both are true, both are real, both are love. To expect grief to follow a schedule is to misunderstand it entirely.

The work of grief is not to erase the past but to keep it alive in a new way. That is why grief can feel like both a wound and a gift. It hurts because someone is gone, but it also reminds us that someone lived, that they mattered, that they loved and were loved. Grief is the shadow cast by love. Without love, there would be no grief. And if grief lasts a lifetime, it is because love lasts a lifetime too.

I once heard a man speak at his wife's memorial. He said, I will grieve her until my last breath, and I am glad for it. Because every tear is a reminder that I was lucky enough to love her. That is the truest expression of grief as love. It is not weakness. It is not failure. It is gratitude in the shape of sorrow.

In learning to see grief this way, we can also learn to support others differently. Instead of telling them to be strong, we can remind them that tears are strength. Instead of avoiding the name of the one who died, we can say it often, knowing it comforts rather than wounds. Instead of disappearing after the funeral, we can show up weeks and months later, because grief lingers and so must love.

There is no end to grief, just as there is no end to love. But there is transformation. Over time, grief shifts. The sharp edges soften. The waves become less violent. The tears come alongside laughter. Memory becomes less painful and more tender. It never disappears, but it becomes integrated into the rhythm of life.

When we stop treating grief as an enemy and begin to see it as love, we give ourselves permission to mourn fully and to live fully. We allow sorrow and joy to sit side by side. We accept that tears and laughter can come in the same breath. We understand that to grieve deeply is to have loved deeply, and that is something to be honored, not hidden.

In the end, grief is not about endings. It is about continuations. It is about carrying love forward into a new chapter. It is about recognizing that someone's absence can still shape presence. It is about learning to live with an ache that never goes away because the love that caused it never goes away.

Live Fully. Leave Wisely.

Grief is love, changed but unbroken. It is the last gift of a bond that was real, and it is the proof that death cannot erase what life once held. To honor grief is to honor love. To carry grief is to carry love. To speak of grief openly is to say, love was here, and love is still here.

Chapter

9

REDUCING THE STRESS

When death comes, it does not arrive politely. It enters like a storm, scattering everything we thought was stable. The routines of daily life vanish, replaced by hospital visits, phone calls, paperwork, and decisions that feel impossible to make. Families who are already carrying the weight of grief find themselves also carrying the weight of logistics, legalities, and obligations that do not pause for sorrow. The combination can feel unbearable. Yet it does not have to be this way. There are ways to ease the burden, ways to prepare so that when the storm comes, it does not tear everything apart.

Stress around death comes in many forms. There is the emotional stress of loss, of course, but layered on top of it are the practical stresses of what to do next. Who calls the funeral home. What kind of service should be held. Who pays the bills. What happens to the house, the bank accounts, the car. These questions arrive all at once, often in the very moments when clarity is most difficult to summon. In the middle of shock, someone is asked to choose caskets or write obituaries. In the middle of grief, someone is asked to sign papers or negotiate with creditors. It is no wonder that so many families describe the days after a death as a blur of confusion and exhaustion.

I once knew a man who described the days following his mother's death as a second kind of trauma. He had expected grief. He had expected sadness. What he had not expected was to be sitting in a funeral home less than twenty-four hours later, asked to choose between ten different casket models with prices that ranged from painful to impossible. He said the salespeople spoke quickly, as though speed would make the decision easier. He nodded and signed because he did not have the strength to argue, then later regretted it for years. His grief was compounded by guilt and by debt. The stress did not end with the funeral. It stretched on for years as bills arrived and decisions were second guessed.

This is the kind of stress that preparation can ease. Not by taking away grief, which cannot be avoided, but by reducing the noise that surrounds it. When wishes are clear, when plans are in place, when documents are ready, families are freed to focus on what matters most. They are freed to sit together, to share memories, to support one another, instead of scrambling through file cabinets or arguing in funeral parlors.

I met another family whose experience was the opposite. Their father had spent his last years quietly organizing his affairs. He left a binder with all his documents, his wishes for medical care, even notes about his funeral. When he died, his children wept, but they did not fight. They did not scramble. They opened the binder and followed his voice. One of them told me, our grief was still heavy, but the weight of confusion was gone. That was his last gift to us. He gave us the freedom to grieve without chaos.

Stress does not only come from the big decisions. It comes from the countless small ones as well. Who notifies distant relatives. Who cancels subscriptions. Who remembers to close social media accounts. Who handles the pets, the mail, the garden. In the fog of loss, these small details feel overwhelming. When they are not planned for, they pile up into a mountain. But when they are written down, when they are anticipated, they become manageable.

Stress also rises from family dynamics. Death does not erase old wounds. In fact, it often magnifies them. Siblings who have not spoken in years may be forced into a room together. Spouses may disagree about money. Children may resent each other's choices. Without guidance, these tensions can explode into lasting conflict. I have seen families fracture over decisions as small as who spoke at the funeral or who received a photo album. These fractures do not always heal. Grief becomes entangled with anger, and love is overshadowed by resentment.

Yet I have also seen the opposite. Families who, because of preparation, are able to stay united. Parents who wrote letters not only with instructions but with blessings, urging their children to remain close. Siblings who found peace in knowing that the hard choices were already made. In these families, grief still hurt, but stress did not break their bonds. They leaned on each other instead of pulling apart. Preparation had not only reduced stress, it had preserved love.

There is also the stress that comes from uncertainty about meaning. What kind of funeral best reflects a life. What words should be spoken. What music should be played. Without guidance, families often turn to what is easiest or most common, even if it feels hollow. But when someone leaves instructions, even simple ones, the service becomes a reflection of who they were. I remember one woman who had written that she wanted her funeral to end with everyone singing her favorite Beatles song. Her children honored that request, and the room filled with voices both joyful and tearful. The stress of planning disappeared because the plan was already there. What remained was the simple act of honoring her.

Stress is not only emotional. It is physical. Studies show that those who are grieving often suffer from insomnia, fatigue, headaches, even weakened immune systems. Add the demands of paperwork, financial negotiations, and family conflict, and the toll on the body becomes immense. Preparation reduces that toll. It creates space for rest. It allows families to care for themselves as well as for each other.

One of the most overlooked forms of stress is financial. Funerals are expensive. Medical bills can be staggering. Debts do not vanish with death. Families are often blindsided by costs they did not anticipate. The pressure to spend, combined with the guilt of appearing cheap in the face of loss, pushes many into debt. But when financial plans are made ahead of time, when accounts are organized, when instructions are given, families are spared from decisions made under emotional duress. They are spared from being sold to while they are still in shock. They are given the peace of knowing that the choices they make are aligned with what their loved one wanted, not with what they felt pressured to buy.

To reduce stress is not only to protect loved ones from chaos. It is to honor them. It is to say, I cared enough to make this easier for you. It is to recognize that grief is heavy enough without adding confusion, conflict, and exhaustion. It is to leave a gift of peace in the midst of sorrow.

Paul Fried

Stress cannot be eliminated entirely. Death is disruptive by its very nature. But it can be softened. It can be managed. And most importantly, it can be anticipated. The act of preparing, of writing wishes, of organizing documents, of speaking openly, is an act of love. It is love in its most practical form. It is love that says, when the time comes, you will not have to carry this alone.

In every family I have met, the difference is clear. Where there is silence, there is stress. Where there is preparation, there is space for love. We cannot choose to spare our families from grief, but we can choose to spare them from chaos. And that choice is one of the most meaningful legacies we can leave.

Chapter

10

CONVERSATIONS THAT MATTER

Most of us spend our lives in conversation, but so few of those conversations touch the subjects that matter most. We talk about the weather, the errands that need running, the shows we are watching, the meals we have eaten, the gossip of neighbors or coworkers. We fill our days with words, but often we avoid the words that truly matter, the ones that cut to the heart of who we are and what we want for our lives and for our deaths. These conversations are difficult, but they are also essential. They are the conversations that open doors to peace, to clarity, to connection. Without them, families stumble in the dark when the hardest moments arrive.

It is not that people do not want to have these conversations. It is that they are afraid. Afraid of upsetting loved ones, afraid of sounding morbid, afraid of facing their own mortality. They tell themselves there will be time later, but later rarely comes. I have heard countless stories from families who said, we always meant to talk about it, but we never did. When the moment came, they were left guessing. Guessing what kind of care their loved one wanted, guessing what kind of service would honor them, guessing how to divide responsibilities. Guessing is the cruel opposite of love. It replaces clarity with confusion, peace with stress, unity with conflict.

I remember speaking to a woman whose husband had died suddenly. She told me the hardest part was not his death itself but the silence that preceded it. They had never spoken about what he would want if something happened. She did not know if he wanted to be buried or cremated. She did not know if he wanted a church service or something simple. She made choices in the fog of grief, and years later she still wondered if she had honored him or betrayed him. Every holiday, every anniversary, those doubts returned. His silence had become her burden.

And then there are families who have spoken. I once attended a funeral where the service was filled with music chosen by the person who had died. She had spoken to her children about what songs mattered to her, what readings she loved, what food she wanted served afterward. The funeral was not an act of guessing but of honoring. Her children cried, but they also laughed, because everything felt so true to her spirit. They said it felt like she was there, guiding them through. The difference between those two families was not chance. It was conversation.

The conversations that matter are not only about logistics. They are about values. They are about what makes life worth living. They are about what kind of care feels like dignity. They are about what kind of legacy matters most. Some people find meaning in prolonging life as long as possible, embracing every medical intervention available. Others find meaning in comfort, in quality of days rather than quantity. Neither choice is wrong, but each is deeply personal. Without conversation, those choices remain unknown.

Live Fully. Leave Wisely.

Silence is often mistaken for kindness. People avoid speaking of death because they do not want to upset their children, or their spouse, or their parents. They think silence protects. In truth, silence does the opposite. It leaves the ones they love most to face the hardest choices without guidance. It leaves them vulnerable to conflict, to guilt, to regret. To speak openly may be uncomfortable, but it is the greater kindness. It gives the people you love the gift of clarity when they will need it most.

These conversations are not only for the elderly or the ill. They are for everyone. Death does not check a calendar before it arrives. Accidents happen, diagnoses come, time runs out unexpectedly. To wait until later is to gamble with the people you love. I once spoke with a young woman whose husband died in his thirties. She said, we had talked about everything except this. We were too young to think it mattered. But it did matter. It mattered because when the unthinkable happened, she was left alone to decide. She told me she would give anything to go back and have one honest conversation.

The truth is that these conversations do not have to be heavy. They do not have to be clinical. They can be woven into life with gentleness, with humor, with love. A father can tell his children over dinner, if I go before you, play my favorite song and tell the story of how I embarrassed myself at that wedding. A mother can say, if I cannot live at home, promise me you will bring me my gardenias. A spouse can say, I do not want machines, but I do want music. These are not dark conversations. They are conversations about love, about dignity, about being known.

The hardest part is beginning. People stumble on the first words. But once the door is opened, the conversations often flow more easily than expected. Families discover that instead of pulling them into despair, the conversations bring relief. They laugh, they tell stories, they remember, they connect. What begins as a talk about death often becomes a deeper talk about life.

In some cultures, these conversations are not avoided but embraced. In parts of Africa, families speak openly about death, and funeral planning is part of the rhythm of community life. In Mexico, Día de los Muertos is a time when families not only remember the dead but also speak of their own wishes, knowing that death is part of the cycle of living. In Bhutan, people are taught to contemplate death daily, not as something morbid but as something that sharpens appreciation for life. By contrast, in modern America, we whisper, we avoid, we pretend. And in doing so, we make grief heavier and love harder to carry.

To create conversations that matter, one must begin with honesty. Honesty about fear. Honesty about values. Honesty about hopes. These conversations may reveal disagreements, but those disagreements are better discovered now than in the chaos of a hospital waiting room. They may reveal pain, but that pain is better healed now than multiplied later. They may reveal love, and that love is better spoken now than assumed forever.

There is a particular power in hearing someone you love speak directly about their wishes. It transforms decisions from burdens into acts of devotion. When a daughter says, my father told me he wanted this, the choice feels like love, not like guessing. When a son says, my mother told me she wanted this, the choice feels like honoring, not like gambling. Conversations create anchors. In the storm of grief, they give families something to hold on to.

Some people believe that writing things down is enough, that documents can replace words. But documents, though necessary, cannot capture tone, cannot convey love, cannot heal wounds. Words spoken face to face carry meaning that no paper can.

A handwritten directive may say do not resuscitate, but only a conversation can explain why that choice reflects dignity. A legal will may distribute possessions, but only a conversation can explain what those objects meant. Paper records decisions. Words record love.

In the end, conversations that matter are conversations of love. They are the chance to say what should not be left unsaid. They are the chance to replace silence with connection. They are the chance to ensure that when the time comes, the people you love most will not be left guessing. They are not easy conversations, but they are sacred ones.

We cannot control death. We cannot control the timing or the manner in which it arrives. But we can control whether we meet it with silence or with speech. We can control whether we leave our families with confusion or with clarity. We can control whether we let fear dictate silence or let love inspire words. The conversations that matter are waiting for us to begin them.

And perhaps the greatest truth of all is that these conversations, though they are about death, are also about life. They remind us of what we value, of who we love, of what we want our days to mean. They remind us to live more intentionally, to forgive sooner, to love more openly. They remind us that one day will be our last day, and because of that, today is precious.

To speak of death is not to diminish life. It is to honor it. To have conversations that matter is to choose love over fear, clarity over silence, connection over avoidance. One day, your family will sit together and remember you. The story they tell will be shaped by the words you spoke or the silence you left. Begin the conversation now. Begin it with love. Because these conversations do not only prepare us for dying. They prepare us for living well, fully, and honestly.

Chapter

11

STARTING SMALL

When people think about end of life planning, they often imagine it as a mountain that must be climbed in a single day. They picture stacks of papers, complex legal documents, difficult conversations, and overwhelming emotions. The very thought of beginning feels paralyzing. So they put it off. They tell themselves that one day, when things calm down, when they feel ready, when life is less busy, they will tackle it. That day rarely arrives. Life never truly slows down. The result is that important decisions remain unmade, and the silence grows heavier with each passing year.

The truth is that planning does not have to begin with a mountain. It can begin with a single step. Starting small is not only easier, it is often more effective. The process of preparing for death is less about one grand act and more about many small acts accumulated over time. A conversation here, a note written there, a single document filled out and set aside. Piece by piece, clarity emerges. Piece by piece, the mountain becomes a series of hills, each one manageable.

Live Fully. Leave Wisely.

I once knew a woman who dreaded the idea of writing a will. She imagined hours with a lawyer, complicated forms, and fees she could not afford. For years she avoided it. Then one evening she sat down at her kitchen table with a pen and paper and simply wrote a letter. In it she listed the people she wanted to inherit her possessions, and she explained why. It was not legally binding, but it was a start. That small act gave her the courage to do more. A few months later she found a simple will template online, filled it out, and had it notarized. What once felt impossible became manageable because she started small.

The same is true of conversations. Families often avoid talking about death because the idea of a big, formal conversation feels too heavy. They imagine gathering everyone in a room, sitting in silence, and trying to force the words out. But conversations do not have to begin that way. They can start with a single sentence. A father telling his daughter while driving, if anything ever happens to me, know that I want things to be simple. A mother saying over dinner, I hope you remember that I would prefer to be at home if I get sick. These small sentences, spoken casually, begin to open the door. Once the door is open, larger conversations can follow.

There is power in realizing that every small step counts. Writing down a list of accounts and passwords may not feel like much, but to a family left behind, it is a lifeline. Choosing a healthcare proxy may feel like a simple decision, but it can save loved ones from conflict and confusion. Telling a spouse your wishes for music at your funeral may seem like a small detail, but when the time comes, it becomes a source of comfort and connection.

I met a man who described his mother's passing as peaceful not because everything had been perfectly arranged but because she had left enough small clues. She had not filled out every form, but she had written notes in her Bible. She had not preplanned the funeral, but she had told her children the hymns she loved. These small steps gave the family guidance. They did not feel abandoned. They felt cared for. He said, she may not have finished everything, but she started enough. And that was a gift.

Starting small also helps overcome fear. When people imagine tackling everything at once, they often freeze. But when they take one step, they realize it was not as hard as they thought. That success gives them courage to take another step. Momentum builds. A person who begins by choosing a healthcare proxy may later feel ready to complete an advance directive. A person who starts by writing down their funeral song choices may later sit down with their children for a longer talk. Each step builds confidence. Each step reduces fear.

There is also something deeply human about small steps. Life itself is built of small steps. We do not live in grand moments alone. We live in daily choices, daily habits, daily conversations. Preparing for death should reflect that same rhythm. To start small is to align with the way life actually unfolds.

One of the greatest obstacles to planning is perfectionism. People tell themselves that if they cannot do everything, they should do nothing. They wait until they can afford a lawyer, until they can block out a whole weekend, until they feel completely ready. But perfectionism is the enemy of preparation. Small steps are always better than no steps. A simple note is better than silence. An informal conversation is better than none at all. A basic will is better than leaving nothing. Families do not need perfection. They need guidance, however modest.

I recall a story of a man who died suddenly, leaving behind a wife and three children. He had not written a formal will, but he had left a single note in his desk. In it he listed a few wishes, including that his children be cared for by his brother if anything happened. That note, though not legally binding, gave his wife the clarity she needed. It gave her a direction. It gave her peace. Later she told me, it was not perfect, but it was enough. He started, and that mattered more than anything.

The beauty of starting small is that it creates space for growth. Once a person begins, they often find themselves thinking more openly about death, more willing to talk, more able to prepare. What once seemed frightening becomes less so. What once seemed overwhelming becomes simply another part of living. Death does not feel like an enemy to be avoided but a reality to be acknowledged with honesty.

In families, small starts can ripple outward. One person's decision to begin often inspires others. A mother who fills out an advance directive may prompt her children to do the same. A father who writes down funeral wishes may encourage his siblings to share theirs. Small steps create momentum not only for individuals but for communities. They normalize preparation. They make it less strange, less frightening, less avoided.

The work of starting small is also about love. To write a note, to share a sentence, to choose a proxy, to organize a file, these may seem like small acts. But in truth, they are profound. They say, I thought of you. I wanted to make this easier. I wanted to leave you with clarity instead of confusion. Love is not always expressed in grand gestures. It is most often expressed in small, consistent acts. The same is true in death as in life.

For anyone who feels overwhelmed by the thought of planning, the invitation is simple. Do not aim to finish everything today. Aim to begin something today. Write down a single wish. Share a single sentence. Choose a single person to carry your voice. Place one stone at the base of the mountain. Tomorrow, place another. The mountain will not seem so high. The silence will not seem so heavy. The fear will not seem so great.

In the end, it is not about how quickly the planning is finished. It is about whether the planning is begun. Families do not remember whether every form was filled out perfectly. They remember whether there was guidance, whether there was clarity, whether there was love. And all of that can begin with a single, small step.

When the time comes, and it always does, those small steps will not feel small at all. They will feel like lifelines. They will feel like love. They will feel like the difference between chaos and peace, between silence and clarity, between regret and gratitude.

Starting small is not a compromise. It is the beginning of love made visible. It is the path from avoidance to preparation, from fear to courage, from silence to words that matter. It is the way we honor our lives and the people we love most.

Chapter

12

KEEPING IT SIMPLE

There is a temptation when facing the idea of death and planning for it to overcomplicate everything. We live in a culture that prizes complexity. We believe that if something is important it must also be elaborate, filled with details, protocols, and layers of formality. We see this in the way funerals are often arranged with packages that include flowers, music, transportation, memorial cards, and endless decisions that feel less like honoring a life and more like managing an event. We see it in the way people become tangled in legal documents, multiple revisions of wills, and elaborate estate plans that sometimes leave families confused rather than comforted.

The truth is that most people do not need complexity. They need clarity. They need direction. They need simplicity. Keeping it simple does not mean careless or incomplete. It means reducing the noise so that the essentials remain visible. It means ensuring that when the time comes, families are not drowning in details but anchored in love and guidance.

Paul Fried

I once knew a man who worked for years on an elaborate estate plan. He hired multiple attorneys. He spent countless hours drafting and redrafting. He created binders filled with documents, each one more complicated than the last. When he died his children opened those binders and found themselves paralyzed. They could not make sense of it all. They fought over interpretations. They hired more lawyers. Years passed before anything was resolved. For all his effort, the man left behind not peace but confusion. He thought complexity would mean protection. In reality, it became a burden.

Contrast that with the woman who left a single handwritten letter. It outlined her wishes in plain language. She said who she wanted to care for her grandchildren. She said she wanted a simple service with music from her church choir. She said she wanted her ashes scattered in the river where she used to fish with her husband. That letter was short. It was not written in legal jargon. But it was clear. Her family read it together after her death and felt guided. They knew what she wanted. They felt her presence in her words. They did not argue. They did not need to. The simplicity of her instructions gave them space to grieve, to laugh, to remember.

Simplicity carries dignity. When we strip away the unnecessary, we uncover what matters most. The family needs to know the wishes. They need to know how to honor them. They do not need complexity that obscures the heart of the matter. Keeping it simple is not only easier for those who plan, it is a final gift to those left behind.

There is another dimension to this. Complexity often comes from fear. People feel that if they cover every possible scenario, they will be safe. If they create enough rules and details, nothing will go wrong. But death will never be completely safe. It will never unfold exactly as imagined. Complexity cannot protect us from grief. What it often does instead is distract us from the truth. Families do not gather to admire the intricacy of plans. They gather to remember and to grieve. What they need is not a manual but a map, not a binder but a compass.

I recall speaking with a hospice nurse who had seen hundreds of families navigate the death of a loved one. She told me that the most peaceful families were not the ones with elaborate plans. They were the ones with simple, clear instructions. She said that too much detail often left families feeling they had failed. If every aspect was spelled out and something went wrong, they carried guilt. Simpler instructions left room for grace. They gave families the freedom to make decisions without feeling like they had broken rules. Simplicity did not limit love. It expanded it.

There is also a spiritual truth in simplicity. At the end of life, much of what we chase falls away. Money, possessions, achievements, reputations, they shrink in importance. What rises to the surface are relationships, values, memories. These are simple things. They do not require elaborate planning. They require honesty and clarity. A person who spends time writing a single letter of love to their children may leave behind more comfort than a person who spends months arranging complicated logistics.

Keeping it simple also makes planning accessible. Many people avoid end of life planning because they believe it requires great expense or complicated expertise. But the essentials can be addressed in simple ways. A healthcare proxy can be chosen with a single conversation. Funeral wishes can be written on a single page. Passwords can be listed in a small notebook. None of these require advanced knowledge or endless meetings. They require the willingness to begin. Simplicity lowers the barrier to entry. It makes planning possible for everyone, not just those with resources and time.

There is beauty in simplicity because it reflects life itself. The most meaningful moments are usually the simplest. A laugh shared at a dinner table. A quiet walk with a friend. A child falling asleep on a parent's shoulder. None of these require complexity. They are rich because they are simple. End of life planning should follow that same rhythm.

One family I knew decided to honor their father with a simple graveside service. There was no reception hall, no long list of speakers, no elaborate program. Just a circle of family and friends sharing stories in the open air. Each person spoke from the heart. There were tears and laughter. There was honesty. The family later said it felt truer to him than anything else could have. It was simple, and in its simplicity, it was sacred.

The same applies to possessions. People often spend hours worrying about how to divide belongings. They create complex lists and conditions. But what matters most are not the things themselves but the memories attached to them. Simplicity asks us to see that truth. To say, this necklace goes to you because you always loved it. This book goes to you because you shared it with me. It does not have to be more complicated than that. When families approach inheritance with simplicity, they reduce conflict. They preserve love.

Simplicity is also kinder to those who are grieving. In the fog of loss, even small decisions can feel overwhelming. If the instructions are too complex, families may freeze. They may feel inadequate. They may argue. But when instructions are simple, they can move forward with confidence. They can trust themselves. They can focus on what truly matters, remembering the person they loved.

There is a lesson here for those who are hesitant to begin planning. You do not need to know everything. You do not need to create a flawless plan. You only need to begin with what is clear to you now. Write it down simply. Speak it simply. Let your family know your heart. That is enough to start. More can be added later if needed. But the beginning should be simple.

I once sat with a man in his seventies who had never spoken to his children about his wishes. He felt embarrassed. He felt it was too late. But one afternoon he told them over coffee that he wanted to be cremated and that he wanted his ashes scattered in the mountains where he had hiked all his life. That was all he said. It took less than a minute. His children were relieved. They told him, thank you. It was a simple moment. But it mattered more than he could have imagined.

Simplicity also carries humility. It recognizes that our control is limited. No matter how much we plan, there will always be uncertainties. Keeping things simple allows space for life to unfold as it will. It allows families to adapt. It allows grief to flow naturally. Complexity often tries to dictate every detail. Simplicity accepts that not everything can be controlled. That acceptance is a gift.

In many cultures around the world, simplicity has long been valued in death rituals. In some traditions, bodies are washed and wrapped in cloth without embellishment. In others, families gather for meals rather than formal services. These practices remind us that at the end, it is not grandeur that matters but presence. It is not spectacle that comforts but love. Simplicity connects us back to what has always been true.

We live in an age where everything is marketed, where even grief is commercialized. But families do not need products as much as they need connection. They do not need packages as much as they need clarity. They do not need extravagance as much as they need simplicity. To choose simplicity is to resist a culture that tries to turn death into business. It is to return to the essence of what matters.

Keeping it simple is not about doing less. It is about doing what matters most. It is about choosing clarity over clutter, love over logistics, presence over performance. When we strip away the unnecessary, we leave behind what is essential. And when families are left with what is essential, they can grieve with honesty, remember with joy, and carry forward with peace.

In the end, planning is not about creating the perfect binder or the most elaborate service. It is about giving your family the gift of guidance. And that gift is best delivered simply. A letter. A sentence. A choice spoken aloud. A wish written down. That is enough. It has always been enough.

Chapter

13

UPDATING THE PLAN

When people finally take the courageous step of putting their wishes in writing there is often a sense of relief. It feels as though a heavy burden has been lifted. The hard part is done and the plan exists. But there is a common mistake hidden in that sense of accomplishment. Many people treat their end of life plan as though it were carved into stone, untouchable, unchanging, finished forever. Life, however, does not remain still. Families grow and change. Relationships shift. Circumstances evolve. What felt certain in one decade may feel foreign in the next. To truly honor ourselves and those we love, we must learn not only to create a plan but to revisit it, to update it, to allow it to live and breathe alongside us.

I once spoke with a woman who had created a will shortly after the birth of her first child. She did the responsible thing at the urging of her lawyer. She outlined guardianship. She set up a trust. She even described the kind of funeral she wanted. For years she kept the document in a folder in her desk, untouched. By the time she died unexpectedly, her children were adults, her marriage had ended, and she had remarried. The guardianship she had so carefully chosen no longer made sense. The trust no longer matched her family's reality. Her wishes reflected a life that no longer existed. Her children were left sorting through instructions that belonged to the past. The sadness of losing her was heavy enough. The confusion of outdated wishes made it heavier still.

Updating the plan is not about indecision or wavering. It is about truth. Life changes. What we want at twenty may not be what we want at fifty. A young couple might dream of being buried side by side in a family plot, but decades later they may find peace in the idea of cremation and scattering ashes in the places they loved most. A parent may name a trusted sibling as guardian for their children, only to realize years later that the sibling's health or circumstances make that impossible. A person might begin with a desire for aggressive medical treatment, then, after watching a loved one suffer through prolonged interventions, choose a different path. None of these changes are wrong. They are simply honest. Updating the plan is an act of staying faithful to the life we are living now, not the one we lived years ago.

There is a sense of humility in this. Many of us want to believe that once we have made a decision, it is final. We crave certainty. But life has never promised us certainty. What it offers instead is movement, growth, and constant change. To resist updating our plans is to resist the reality of our own evolving selves. To embrace updating is to accept that love, wisdom, and clarity deepen with time.

I remember an elderly man who kept a small notebook in his desk drawer. Every few years he would pull it out, read through it, and make adjustments. Sometimes he changed a name. Sometimes he added a few lines about music or readings. Sometimes he crossed out an old idea that no longer felt important. The notebook was not elegant or official. But it was alive. It reflected the story of a life that continued to grow. When he died, his children found not only instructions but also a record of his changing journey. They said it felt like a conversation with him through the years. It reminded them that he had continued to think of them, to love them, to prepare for them.

There is also a practical truth here. Laws change. Financial situations change. Medical options change. What was once legally sound may become outdated. What was once financially wise may later become impossible. To never revisit a plan is to risk leaving behind something broken. A simple review every few years can prevent years of frustration for loved ones.

Updating the plan is not just about documents. It is also about conversations. Families need to hear from us, not just once, but throughout the journey. A conversation with a spouse at thirty may be remembered, but a new conversation at sixty may carry very different wisdom. Children who are too young to understand when we first speak may need to hear again when they are adults. Conversations, like documents, need to be renewed, refreshed, and kept alive.

Some resist updating because they fear it will be overwhelming. They imagine having to start from scratch, to go through every detail again. But often updating is simple. It may be as small as writing a note that says I no longer want this, I prefer this. It may be as simple as telling a child where the updated papers are kept. It may be as quick as changing the name of a proxy or writing down a new wish. Updating does not require perfection. It requires attention.

There is wisdom in making updating a ritual. Some people choose to revisit their plan every New Year as part of reflecting on the year that has passed. Others do it on their birthday as a reminder of the gift of time. Some do it after major life events, a marriage, a birth, a divorce, a move. Whatever the rhythm, the act of returning to the plan becomes a practice in itself, a way of staying aligned with truth and love.

I knew a woman who updated her plan every time she returned from a long trip. She said travel reminded her of how fragile life is, how uncertain. Each time she came home she would sit with her plan for an hour, making sure it still spoke for her. Her family laughed about it, but when she died suddenly they were grateful. Her plan was not only complete, it was current. They had no doubt about what she wanted because she had kept it alive.

Updating the plan is also a way of teaching the next generation. Children who watch their parents review and revise learn that planning is not a one time burden but a normal part of life. They learn that love is not rigid but responsive. They learn that caring for family includes the humility to keep instructions fresh. In this way updating is not only for the benefit of the present family but for the shaping of how future generations will understand responsibility and love.

There is a story I will never forget of a family who found an envelope in their mother's desk after she passed. It was labeled Updated Plan 2020. Inside were her clear wishes, written only months before her death. They said the greatest comfort was not just that the plan existed, but that it was recent. They knew it reflected her true desires at the end of her life. They did not argue. They did not wonder. They felt guided by her voice, even

Live Fully. Leave Wisely.

in her absence. The envelope was not large, not elaborate, but it carried immense peace because it was current.

Simplicity plays a role here too. Updating does not mean adding more and more detail. It often means refining, clarifying, removing what no longer matters. It is like tending a garden, pulling weeds, trimming branches, allowing the essential plants to flourish. The plan grows not by becoming more complicated but by becoming clearer. Each update is a chance to ask, what still matters, what no longer does, what has changed, what remains true.

We sometimes avoid updating because it forces us to admit that time is passing. To open the plan is to acknowledge that we are closer to the end than we once were. But this truth is not meant to frighten us. It is meant to focus us. Updating is a way of saying, I am still here, I am still choosing, I am still guiding. It is not an admission of defeat but a declaration of love.

I think of the mother who updated her plan after her first grandchild was born. She added a note about how she wanted her grandchildren to be cared for if something happened to their parents. She included words of blessing for them. She wrote about her hopes for their futures. Her children said those words became treasures, not because they were legally binding, but because they carried her voice. Her willingness to update gave her family a gift they never expected, a piece of her love that stretched into the next generation.

There is also peace in knowing that an updated plan removes guilt. When families are left with outdated instructions they often second guess themselves. They wonder if they are doing the right thing. They feel torn between following old wishes and honoring what they believe their loved one would have wanted later. But when a plan is current, there is no room for doubt. The family can move forward with confidence, knowing they are carrying out what is true.

Updating is, at its heart, about presence. It is about refusing to let the plan grow stale. It is about being present to our own lives and to the people we love. It is about keeping our final words aligned with our present hearts.

So if you have already created a plan, know that you have done something remarkable. But do not stop there. Make a promise to yourself and to your family that you will return to it, revisit it, breathe life into it again and again. Let it evolve as you evolve. Let it remain a reflection of who you are and what you value now, not only who you were years ago.

Because a plan is not just a piece of paper. It is a bridge between you and the ones who will carry your memory. And a bridge, like anything built to endure, needs care. It needs attention. It needs to be kept strong, not only when it is first built but throughout the years.

To update the plan is to say, I am still here. I am still thinking of you. I am still preparing to love you, even when I can no longer speak. That is the gift. That is the act of love.

Chapter

14

THE BUSINESS OF DEATH

There is a moment that comes for almost every family, usually within hours of a loved one passing, when the reality of grief collides with the machinery of commerce. The body has not even cooled, tears are still wet on cheeks, yet decisions must be made. Where will the body go. Which funeral home should be called. What package will be selected. How will it be paid for. It is a collision between the most human experience and one of the most entrenched industries in modern life. Death, in America, is not only a personal passage. It is also a business. And like any business it has its costs, its profits, its sales techniques, and its culture.

Most people do not think of funerals until they are forced into one. We imagine them vaguely, in soft tones, with flowers and prayers. What we rarely imagine is the reality of the decisions presented in the sterile office of a funeral director. There are forms to sign. There are packages to choose from. There are options that range in price from modest to staggering. A grieving family sits across the table, dazed and exhausted, and someone in a suit gently guides them through a catalog. It is a catalog of grief, priced per casket, per service, per limousine. Few industries operate with such certainty of customers. Everyone dies. Every family must make choices. And in that inevitability lies the foundation of the business of death.

This is not to vilify funeral directors. Many of them enter the profession with genuine compassion, with a calling to care for families in their darkest hours. They know how to move gently. They know how to navigate raw emotion. They know how to create an atmosphere of reverence. But the truth is that they also operate within a system designed for profit. A funeral home must pay staff, maintain facilities, and market services. It must compete with others. It must sell. The tension between compassion and commerce is built into the very walls.

For many families the first shock after a death is not only emotional but financial. Costs can climb quickly, sometimes into tens of thousands of dollars. A casket can cost more than a car. Embalming, flowers, transportation, cemetery fees, headstones, obituaries, receptions, each item adds to the total. It is not uncommon for a grieving spouse or child to feel pressured into spending more than they can afford, simply because it feels like a measure of love. To choose the cheaper option feels like failing the one who has died. To choose simplicity can feel like disrespect. Funeral homes know this, and while many are ethical, the system itself leans toward upselling.

There is a story of a young couple who lost their infant child. They arrived at the funeral home shattered, barely able to speak. The director walked them through options, each one more expensive than the last. They chose a white casket with gold trim, the most costly one available, because in their pain they could not bear the thought of anything less. Years later they admitted they went into debt for that choice. They did not regret honoring their child, but they carried resentment toward a system that profited from their grief. The funeral industry did not kill their child, but it capitalized on the love that death had made raw.

In earlier times death was not outsourced in this way. Families cared for the body themselves. They washed it. They dressed it. They built the coffin. They dug the grave. Death was part of the fabric of life, handled within the community. It was not an industry, it was a ritual. The rise of the funeral business coincided with urbanization, with the professionalization of death care, and with the cultural shift that made death something to be hidden, sanitized, and managed by experts. What was once a family responsibility became a service to be purchased.

There is comfort in professionalism. Funeral directors bring expertise, organization, and structure at a time when families may feel lost. But professionalism has also distanced us from the intimacy of death. We have traded connection for convenience, ritual for transaction. And the cost of that trade is both financial and emotional.

I once sat with a man who had worked as a gravedigger for thirty years. He told me he had seen families ruined by the costs of funerals. He said he never understood why a casket should cost as much as it did. He built simple pine boxes for his own family members, strong and plain, and he believed that was enough. He said he did not measure love in wood or satin, but in presence. Yet he watched as family after family fell into the trap of equating expense with honor. He said the saddest thing was not lowering the casket into the ground, but knowing the family above was burdened with bills they could not pay.

The business of death thrives on silence and avoidance. Because we do not talk about death openly, we do not prepare. And when we are unprepared, we are vulnerable. We make decisions in crisis, guided by guilt and fear. We spend money we do not have. We sign contracts we do not understand. We accept what is offered because we cannot bear the thought of bargaining while grieving. In that moment silence becomes expensive. Avoidance becomes a cost measured not only in money but in peace of mind.

Yet there are families who resist. Some choose direct cremation with no service, the simplest and least expensive option. Others return to home funerals, washing and dressing their loved ones themselves, holding vigils in living rooms. These families are often judged as unconventional, but in truth they are reclaiming what once was normal. They are saying that love does not need a price tag, that presence matters more than packages, that grief does not have to be sold back to them at market rates.

There is also a growing movement toward green burials. Simple shrouds, biodegradable caskets, no embalming, natural settings where bodies return to the earth without chemicals or marble. These choices are not only environmentally friendly, they are often less expensive. They reflect a desire to step outside the machinery of the death business and back into the rhythm of nature. Families who choose them often describe the experience as freeing, more authentic, more aligned with the values of the person who has died.

The challenge is that these alternatives require knowledge and planning. Funeral homes rarely advertise the simplest or cheapest options first. They lead with what is profitable. They frame the conversation around packages rather than individual choices. Unless families know their rights and their options, they may never realize there are other paths. And so part of reclaiming simplicity in death is education, conversation, and preparation.

There is an irony here. The business of death often justifies itself as easing the burden on families. And in some ways it does. But in others it creates burdens of its own. Financial debt. Lingering resentment. The sense that grief was commercialized. Families deserve better. They deserve transparency, honesty, and choice. They deserve the chance to separate love from expense.

I remember a family who chose to gather in their backyard for a memorial service. They printed photographs. They cooked favorite meals. They told stories late into the night. There was no invoice at the end, no sales pitch, no catalog. There was only presence, laughter, tears, and memory. When asked later how they felt about their choice, they said it was the truest thing they could have done. Their grief had not been packaged. It had been lived.

The business of death will not disappear. There will always be need for professionals, for funeral homes, for cemeteries. But families can learn to navigate this system without being consumed by it. They can prepare in advance, making choices when their minds are clear rather than clouded by loss. They can speak openly with loved ones, removing the burden of guesswork. They can seek simplicity when the industry offers complexity. They can remember that love is measured not in dollars but in presence, in memory, in care.

To keep death from becoming purely a business, we must reclaim our role in it. We must bring death back into conversation, back into family, back into community. We must be willing to talk about what we want and what we do not want. We must teach our children that death is not only an industry but a part of life. And when the time comes, we must be ready to walk into those offices, catalogs in hand, and say with clarity, we know what matters and it is not always what is most expensive.

The business of death is powerful because it operates in the shadows of grief. The way to weaken its hold is to bring light. To prepare. To speak. To remember that while death may be inevitable, how we respond to it remains a choice. We can choose complexity or simplicity. We can choose to spend or to preserve. We can choose to measure love in money or in memory. And the choice we make becomes not only a reflection of us but a legacy for those we leave behind.

In the end the business of death is only as strong as our silence. When we speak, when we prepare, when we reclaim, it loses its power. And what remains is not an invoice but a memory, not a transaction but a story, not debt but love.

Chapter

15

THE DIGITAL AFTERLIFE

Not long ago, the only traces people left behind were physical. A box of letters in the attic. A wedding album in the living room. A drawer full of old bills or receipts. Death meant those tangible things remained while the person was gone. But today, much of who we are exists not in drawers or boxes but in the vast, invisible world of the internet. We have social media pages, email accounts, online banking, cloud storage filled with photographs, playlists, passwords, and entire conversations that never touched paper. When a person dies now, what they leave behind is not only a body and belongings but a digital shadow that lingers in the world long after the funeral. This is what we call the digital afterlife, and it is one of the most unspoken yet pressing questions of our age.

I once knew a woman whose daughter died unexpectedly in her twenties. In the weeks that followed, she would sit late at night scrolling through her daughter's social media pages. There were photographs of vacations, silly selfies, messages exchanged with friends. People continued to write on her daughter's wall as though she might respond. They left birthday greetings, anniversary notes, even inside jokes. The mother said it felt like her daughter was still there, in some small way, still present in the pixels and the words. It brought comfort but also confusion. Should she leave the page active. Should she ask for it to be memorialized. Should she delete it entirely. Each option felt like a new kind of loss. The digital afterlife was a space she never imagined having to navigate, and yet it became the place where her grief played out.

This is one of the strange truths of our time. Death used to mean final silence. Now it often means a form of digital presence that lingers indefinitely. Some families treasure this presence, returning to messages and photographs as if visiting a gravesite. Others find it haunting, unable to move on while digital reminders appear in feeds and notifications. The digital afterlife is not good or bad in itself. It is simply real. And like any part of death, it requires thought, preparation, and clarity.

For many people the digital afterlife is overwhelming because we have built lives online without considering how they will end. We create accounts and passwords for every service, from shopping to banking to streaming, often without writing them down. We store photographs in clouds we cannot touch. We keep conversations in platforms that require credentials. When death comes, families often find themselves locked out. They cannot access bank accounts, they cannot retrieve family photos, they cannot even cancel subscriptions. What was once convenience becomes complication.

There is a story of a man who died leaving behind dozens of online accounts, none of which his wife could access. She spent months calling companies, sending death certificates, waiting on hold for hours. In some cases she was told that without the password she would never gain access. Thousands of photographs

Live Fully. Leave Wisely.

were lost, along with years of family history. The husband had not meant to create this burden. He simply never thought about it. But his silence in the digital realm became another form of inheritance, one filled with frustration and loss.

On the other side I knew a father who left his children a neatly organized document with all his online information. He listed every account, every password, every instruction. When he died, his children were able to close what needed closing, preserve what needed preserving, and retrieve precious photographs and videos. They said it felt like he had taken their hands and walked them through it himself. His foresight gave them not only access but also peace.

The digital afterlife is not only about access. It is also about identity. Our online presence is part of how we are remembered. A Facebook page, an Instagram feed, a YouTube channel, these are modern memorials. They shape how people think of us after we are gone. They can preserve our humor, our creativity, our photographs, even our voice. Some people find great comfort in curating these spaces before death, choosing what remains and what disappears. Others leave it entirely to chance, allowing whatever is online at the moment of death to stand as their final reflection.

Technology companies have begun to recognize this reality. Some offer settings that allow accounts to be memorialized, frozen in place but still visible. Others allow users to designate legacy contacts who can manage the account after death. But few people know these options exist, and fewer still take the time to activate them. As a result, families stumble into the digital afterlife without guidance.

There is an ethical dimension to all of this. Who owns our digital selves after we are gone. Does a company own our emails. Does a family member have the right to read private messages. Should a spouse have access to every corner of our digital lives, even those parts we kept hidden. These questions do not have easy answers. They reveal that the digital afterlife is not only about logistics but about intimacy, privacy, and legacy.

I once spoke with a man who discovered after his wife's death that she had kept journals in a private online account. He struggled with whether to open them. On one hand, they were part of her story. On the other, she had chosen to keep them private in life. In the end he read them and found comfort, but also things that startled him. He said he never knew if he had honored her or betrayed her. The digital afterlife forced him into a moral dilemma he had never expected to face.

The digital afterlife also extends into business. For entrepreneurs and creators, online accounts may hold financial value, from websites to digital storefronts. If no one has access, income streams can vanish overnight. Clients may be left stranded. Projects may collapse. The death of a person can mean the silent death of their digital work as well. Updating plans to include these assets is not simply thoughtful. It is essential.

There is also the question of how technology itself may extend our presence after death. Companies are experimenting with artificial intelligence that can mimic a person's voice or style based on digital records. Some services offer to create avatars or chatbots that respond in the way a deceased person might. This raises profound questions. Does it help or harm the grieving to interact with a digital echo of the dead. Is it a comfort to hear a loved one's voice answering back, or does it blur the line between memory and illusion.

Some families embrace this technology, feeling as though it offers a chance to say goodbye in ways they could not before. Others find it unsettling, even grotesque, as though death itself has been interrupted. The digital afterlife, in this form, is not just about preservation but about simulation. It asks us to decide how much of ourselves we want to leave behind, and in what form.

For most of us, the digital afterlife will not be defined by high technology but by simple questions. Who has our passwords. Which accounts should be closed. Which memories should be preserved. How do we want to be remembered online. These are not complicated questions, but they are rarely asked.

The best approach is often the simplest. Write it down. Tell someone you trust. Decide what should remain and what should be deleted. Make it part of your broader plan, not a separate burden. Families who receive this clarity are spared not only logistical headaches but also emotional confusion. They know what to do. They know what to keep. They know how to honor.

The digital afterlife is here whether we like it or not. Every day we add to it with every post, every photo, every email. The choice is whether we will leave it to chance or shape it with intention. Like every part of death, the difference between chaos and peace is preparation.

We will all die. But our digital selves may live on. The question is not whether they will exist, but how they will reflect us. Will they be scattered fragments that confuse and frustrate our families. Or will they be curated reflections that comfort and guide. That choice is ours to make now, in the living, not in the silence that follows.

Paul Fried

Because in the end the digital afterlife is not about technology at all. It is about love. It is about making sure that what remains of us, in any form, is a gift rather than a burden. It is about remembering that even in the realm of passwords and pixels, the heart of the matter is the same as it has always been. To prepare is to love. To speak is to protect. To plan is to leave behind not confusion, but clarity.

Chapter

16

PLANNING ACROSS CULTURES AND FAITHS

Every culture and every faith tradition has its own way of speaking about death, preparing for it, and honoring it. While death is universal, the rituals that surround it are as diverse as the languages spoken across the world. To talk about planning for the end of life without acknowledging these differences is to miss something essential. Death is not only a personal event. It is also a cultural and spiritual passage, shaped by centuries of tradition and belief.

I once attended a Hindu funeral for a close friend's mother. The ceremony began with the body being washed and dressed by family members, an act of devotion and care. Flowers were placed around her, incense burned, prayers were chanted. Later her body was carried to the cremation ground, where fire was seen not as destruction but as purification, a release of the soul from the body. For her family the rituals brought structure, comfort, and meaning. They did not need to wonder what to do or how to do it. Their culture had already provided the path.

Not long after I attended a Jewish funeral, and it could not have been more different in tone yet it carried the same power. The body was not embalmed. It was placed in a plain wooden casket, simple and unadorned, a reminder that death equalizes all. The service was held quickly, within twenty four hours, with prayers recited in Hebrew that had been spoken for generations. There was no attempt to hide grief. People wailed openly, tore their clothing, and spoke honestly about their sorrow. The rituals reminded everyone that death was not to be softened or disguised. It was to be met directly, with honesty and reverence.

These differences illustrate something profound. There is no single correct way to plan for death. There are only ways that are authentic to the values, beliefs, and traditions of the individual and the community. To honor death well we must honor culture and faith.

In Christian traditions, funerals often take the form of a celebration of life. The body may be embalmed, dressed, and displayed for visitation. Services are frequently held in churches with hymns, readings from scripture, and sermons focused on hope, resurrection, and eternal life. In some communities the funeral is followed by a feast, a gathering of family and friends to share food and memory. The message is one of continuity, that death is not an end but a passage into something greater.

In Muslim communities, the rituals are shaped by an equally powerful but very different set of beliefs. The body is washed and shrouded in white cloth, emphasizing equality and simplicity. Burial happens quickly, usually within twenty four hours, and cremation is not permitted. The grave is oriented toward Mecca, prayers are said, and the community gathers to support the family. The emphasis is on humility, submission to God, and the belief that the soul continues its journey beyond the grave.

In some African cultures, funerals are not quiet affairs but vibrant community events. There is singing and dancing, sometimes for days. Death is not seen as the end of relationship but as a continuation, with ancestors watching over the living. The community carries the family through ritual, and grief is shared openly.

In Mexico, Día de los Muertos turns mourning into celebration. Families create altars in their homes filled with photographs, favorite foods, and mementos of the deceased. They visit gravesites, decorate them with flowers and candles, and invite the dead to return for a day. The boundary between life and death is softened, blurred, and transformed into something that feels less like finality and more like reunion.

In Buddhist traditions, death is often seen as part of the cycle of samsara, the endless round of birth, death, and rebirth. Funerals may include chanting, offerings, and prayers for the deceased to achieve a favorable rebirth. The emphasis is on impermanence and the idea that clinging to what has passed brings suffering. Death is not a failure but a reminder of the transience of all things.

For Indigenous peoples across the world, death rituals are deeply tied to land, ancestors, and community. Some tribes in North America view death as a return to the earth and to the spirit world. Ceremonies may involve drumming, singing, and storytelling, with the community gathering not only to grieve but also to ensure the safe passage of the spirit. The emphasis is on connection, on the continuity of life beyond what can be seen.

All of these traditions highlight the same truth. Planning for death is never just practical. It is spiritual, cultural, communal. When families prepare without acknowledging the cultural or faith context, they risk creating rituals that feel hollow. When they lean into tradition, even if only in part, they draw strength from centuries of wisdom.

I once spoke with a man who had grown up in a Christian household but had later identified as agnostic. He never told his family what he wanted for his funeral. When he died, his parents held a church service with hymns and scripture readings. His friends, who knew him differently, said it felt false. They wished he had spoken about his wishes so that they could have honored him in a way that reflected his truth. His silence left his family to fall back on tradition, but it created tension and confusion.

Contrast that with a woman I knew who blended traditions intentionally. She had grown up Catholic but had been influenced by Buddhist practices later in life. Before her death she wrote that she wanted a funeral Mass followed by a meditation circle. She wanted the rosary prayed, but she also wanted bells rung in silence. Her family carried out her instructions with care, and the service became something unique, reflecting her life and her journey. It was authentic because it was hers.

Planning across cultures and faiths is also essential in families that are themselves diverse. Today it is not uncommon for spouses to come from different traditions, or for children to move away from the faith of their parents. In these cases, conversations are even more important. Which traditions will be honored. How will rituals be blended. What matters most to each person. Without these conversations families are left to guess, and guesses can lead to conflict.

There is also the reality of migration and diaspora. Many families live far from their ancestral homes. When death comes, there are decisions about whether to bury locally or return the body to the homeland. These are not only logistical choices but emotional ones, tied to identity and belonging. For some, being buried in the soil of ancestors is nonnegotiable. For others, being near living family matters more. These are difficult choices that require clarity long before the moment of crisis.

Planning across cultures also invites us to learn from one another. When we look beyond our own traditions, we see new possibilities. We see that grief does not have to be silent, it can be sung. We see that funerals do not have to be rushed, they can last days. We see that death does not have to be hidden, it can be invited into celebration. Learning from other traditions does not mean abandoning our own. It means expanding our imagination of what is possible.

One of the most powerful things I have witnessed is when families create rituals that reflect both tradition and individuality. A family may hold a traditional religious service and then gather afterward for a storytelling circle, each person sharing memories. Another family may follow all the formal customs but add personal touches like playing the deceased's favorite songs. In these moments tradition provides the structure, but love provides the detail. The combination is often more meaningful than either alone.

The lesson is clear. When planning, we must not only ask about wills and medical directives. We must also ask about faith and culture. We must ask which rituals matter, which beliefs give comfort, which traditions should be carried forward. These are not small details. They are the heart of what it means to honor someone fully.

Death has always been one of the greatest mirrors of culture. It shows what we value, what we fear, what we hope for beyond life. Planning across cultures and faiths is not just about respecting diversity. It is about understanding that in death, as in life, we are shaped by the stories and traditions that came before us. To prepare well is to honor that inheritance.

And yet there is also room for evolution. Cultures shift. Faith practices adapt. Individuals carve their own paths. Planning is not about rigidly adhering to rules. It is about choosing what feels authentic and meaningful. Sometimes that means following every tradition carefully. Sometimes it means blending, adapting, or even creating new rituals. What matters is that the choices are intentional and clear.

In the end, planning across cultures and faiths teaches us that death is both universal and particular. Universal in that we all face it. Particular in that we each approach it through the lens of our own stories, beliefs, and communities. To plan without acknowledging culture and faith is to plan only halfway. To plan with them is to create something whole, something rooted, something true.

When the time comes, families deserve not only legal documents and logistical instructions. They deserve rituals that feel authentic, prayers that feel familiar, and ceremonies that reflect the life that was lived. They deserve the comfort of knowing they are walking a path shaped by generations. They deserve the freedom to grieve in ways that resonate with their hearts.

And so, in planning, let us remember that death is not simply about closing accounts or distributing possessions. It is about crossing a threshold. It is about honoring ancestors. It is about weaving personal stories into cultural and spiritual tapestries. When we prepare with that awareness, we do more than ease logistics. We preserve meaning. We pass on tradition. We turn silence into song.

Chapter

17

CONVERSATIONS WITH CHILDREN

One of the most tender and most difficult aspects of end of life planning is knowing how and when to speak to children about death. Adults often believe they are protecting children by keeping the subject hidden, by shielding them from conversations that feel heavy, frightening, or too complex. We imagine that childhood should remain untouched by grief, that innocence should be preserved at all costs. Yet in reality children are not strangers to the idea of death. They encounter it in stories, in the loss of pets, in the death of grandparents, even in the cycles of seasons and nature around them. Silence does not protect children. Silence confuses them. What protects children is honest conversation, delivered with love, patience, and trust.

I remember a young boy whose grandmother had died after a long illness. His parents decided not to bring him to the funeral. They told him his grandmother had gone to sleep and was in heaven now, but they gave him no opportunity to see her, to ask questions, or to say goodbye. Months later the boy began waking at night in terror. He told his parents he was afraid to fall asleep because he thought he would not wake up, just as his grandmother had not. The parents realized then that their attempt to soften the truth had created fear. What the boy needed was not avoidance but clarity. He needed someone to explain that death is different from sleep, that his grandmother's body had stopped working, and that he was safe. When those conversations finally happened, his fears eased. He grieved, but he no longer carried the terror of confusion.

Children are perceptive. They know when something is wrong even if no one tells them. They hear whispers in kitchens, they see tears on faces, they sense the heaviness in a room. When adults hide the truth, children often invent their own explanations, and those explanations are rarely comforting. A child may believe they are somehow to blame. They may think they did something wrong that caused the illness or the death. They may build stories in their minds that are far more frightening than the truth. By speaking with honesty, we give children the tools to understand, to ask questions, and to trust the adults around them.

Of course, conversations must be shaped by the age and maturity of the child. A three year old may only need to hear that a body stops working and does not start again, while an older child may ask deeper questions about what happens afterward. The important thing is not to have perfect answers but to respond with openness. It is acceptable to say I do not know. It is acceptable to say different people believe different things. What matters most is that the child feels included, respected, and safe to ask.

I once spoke with a mother who was dying of cancer. She struggled with whether to talk to her children, ages eight and ten, about what was happening. She wanted to protect them. But finally she decided to sit with them one afternoon and explain that her illness was not going away. She told them she loved them and would always love them, even after she was gone. She gave them space to cry and to ask questions. She told them who would care for them and that they would never be alone. Afterward she told me she had expected the conversation to be unbearable, but instead it was strangely peaceful. Her children were sad, but they were also relieved to finally hear the truth spoken aloud. They began to make drawings for her, to write her notes, to spend more time curled in her lap. They did not run from the truth. They leaned into it with love.

Children often approach death with curiosity rather than despair. They ask blunt questions that adults might consider impolite. Where is the body now. Will it smell. Can I see it. Will you die too. These questions may startle adults, but they are healthy. They show that the child is processing reality. When we answer calmly, without judgment, we normalize their curiosity and teach them that death is a part of life, not a forbidden subject.

Avoidance, on the other hand, creates distance. I knew a teenager whose father had died suddenly. No one in the family spoke about it. They avoided the subject entirely. The boy said later that it felt like his father had been erased. He carried anger not only at the loss but at the silence. He wanted to hear stories. He wanted to share memories. He wanted to cry openly. Instead, he learned to shut down, to hide his grief, to pretend. That silence followed him for years.

Conversations with children about death are not only about explaining loss when it happens. They are also about preparing. Just as we encourage children to plan for college or for careers, we can gently encourage them to think about the bigger cycles of life. A parent might say, someday everyone dies, but before that we live fully and love deeply. That simple truth can become a foundation. Children who grow up hearing that death is natural and not shameful are often more resilient when it finally touches them closely.

Rituals can help children process what words cannot. Allowing a child to attend a funeral, to draw a picture and place it in a casket, to light a candle, to tell a story, these actions give them a role in the farewell. They teach that grief is not something to hide but something to share. Children who participate in rituals often feel more at peace than those who are excluded.

At the same time, it is important to recognize that children grieve differently than adults. They may cry one moment and run outside to play the next. Their grief comes in waves, short and intense, rather than long and constant. Adults sometimes mistake this for indifference, but it is simply the way children cope. Talking with them means respecting their rhythms, answering when they ask, holding them when they cry, and giving them permission to return to play when they are ready.

Planning conversations with children also means teaching them about love that endures. A child who hears from a dying parent that love will never end carries that message as a lifelong anchor. A child who is reassured that they will be cared for, that they will not be left alone, gains security that softens fear. These conversations are not about giving every detail. They are about planting seeds of trust.

There is an extraordinary courage in children. I once sat with a twelve year old girl whose mother was dying. She told me she wanted to be there when her mother took her last breath. Her family hesitated, fearing it would scar her. But she insisted. When the time came she sat by the bed, holding her mother's hand, whispering I love you over and over. Later she said she was grateful, that being there gave her peace. She said it was hard, but it was also beautiful. That experience became a source of strength in her life, a reminder that she could face difficult truths with love.

Talking with children about death is not easy, but it is an act of love. It says I trust you. It says you are part of this family in joy and in sorrow. It says you do not need to carry confusion in silence. These conversations may not be perfect. There may be stumbles, tears, awkward moments. But the imperfection is not failure. It is honesty. And honesty is what children need most.

As adults we often underestimate children. We imagine their fragility, but we forget their resilience. They are capable of holding sorrow and joy together in ways adults sometimes cannot. They can laugh in the midst of grief. They can carry love into memory with simplicity. When we invite them into the conversation, we honor their strength.

In the end, conversations with children about death are not only about preparing them. They are also about preparing ourselves. They remind us that truth, spoken with love, is never as frightening as silence. They remind us that grief, shared openly, is always lighter than grief carried alone. And they remind us that even in the hardest moments, the bond of love between parent and child, between grandparent and grandchild, between family and family, is stronger than fear.

When the time comes, and it will, children who have been included in the conversation will not only grieve more honestly. They will also live more fully. They will grow into adults who are not afraid to speak of death, who are not afraid to face it, who understand that it is part of the fabric of life. And that may be the greatest gift we can give them.

Chapter

18

PLANNING FOR CAREGIVERS

When we speak about end of life planning, we often focus on the person who is dying. We ask what they want, where they want to be, what treatments they would accept or refuse, what rituals they hope for, what legacy they want to leave behind. These are essential questions, but there is another side that is often overlooked. Behind every dying person there is usually someone who is caring for them. Sometimes it is a spouse, sometimes a child, sometimes a sibling or a close friend. These caregivers are the quiet heroes of the final chapter. They bear the weight of logistics, emotions, and decisions, often with little support. Planning for caregivers means recognizing their reality and easing their burden.

Caregiving can be an act of profound love. I once met a husband who cared for his wife through five years of Alzheimer's disease. He cooked her meals, bathed her, dressed her, repeated conversations hundreds of times, sat beside her when she no longer knew his name. He told me that love became less about romance and more about presence, less about shared memories and more about simple moments of sitting together in silence.

Yet as moving as his devotion was, it came at a cost. He grew exhausted. He grew lonely. He neglected his own health. He admitted that there were nights when he cried in the bathroom, feeling invisible and overwhelmed. His story is not rare. Caregivers often give everything, and in doing so, they risk losing themselves.

Planning for caregivers is about understanding that love alone is not enough. Structure is needed. Support is needed. Clarity is needed. Too often families drift into caregiving without a map. One person assumes the role by default, usually the one who lives closest or has the fewest work commitments. Others may step back, sometimes out of fear, sometimes out of denial, sometimes because they believe the primary caregiver is stronger. This imbalance creates strain, resentment, and division. A good plan anticipates caregiving not as an afterthought but as a central part of the end of life journey.

One of the most important parts of planning is naming roles. Who will take the lead on medical appointments. Who will handle finances. Who will provide day to day care. Who will step in for respite. These conversations, if had early, prevent confusion later. They also prevent the all too common scenario of one caregiver carrying the entire burden while others remain distant. Clarity is not only a gift to the dying person but to the caregiver who deserves support.

Another essential part of planning is honesty about capacity. Not every family member can or should provide hands on care. A daughter with small children may want to help but may not be able to devote hours each day. A spouse may be aging themselves and unable to lift or manage the physical demands. Planning means acknowledging limits without shame. It means understanding that care can be expressed in many ways. One person may provide direct support. Another may manage finances. Another may bring meals or arrange schedules. Together, these roles weave a net of care that is stronger than any one person could provide alone.

I remember a family where the eldest son was expected to care for his mother full time after her stroke. He tried, but he was also working two jobs to support his own family. He was stretched to breaking. Eventually he collapsed from exhaustion. Only then did the family realize that the burden had been unfairly placed on him. They came together, restructured roles, and created a rotation. His mother was still cared for, but now he was no longer drowning. Planning earlier could have prevented months of silent suffering.

Caregivers also need financial planning. The costs of caregiving are not only emotional but economic. Lost wages, medical expenses, travel, and time all add up. Some caregivers spend their own savings to provide care. Others quit jobs, sacrificing careers. This hidden cost is rarely spoken about, but it is real. Planning means not only discussing inheritance but also considering the needs of the caregiver in the present. If possible, resources should be directed to support them. Insurance, government programs, or shared family contributions can help. What matters is recognizing that caregiving is work, and work should not mean poverty.

There is also the emotional toll. Caregivers often feel isolated. They spend long hours at home, managing medications, cleaning, feeding, watching, waiting. Friends drift away, social lives collapse, personal dreams are put on hold. Depression and anxiety are common. Resentment sometimes bubbles beneath the surface, unspoken but corrosive. Planning must include space for caregivers to breathe, to rest, to find support. This may mean arranging respite care, hiring professionals for certain tasks, or ensuring that other family members step in regularly. It may also mean simply acknowledging the caregiver, thanking them, seeing them. Too many caregivers feel invisible. To plan for them is to say we see you and we value what you are giving.

I think of a daughter who cared for her father through his final months of cancer. She told me that the hardest part was not the physical tasks but the loneliness. She said she sometimes felt forgotten, as though everyone was focused on her father and no one saw her struggle. After he died, people said how brave and strong she had been. She appreciated the words, but she wished someone had said them sooner. She wished someone had asked how she was doing while she was in the middle of it. Her story is a reminder that planning must include not only logistics but compassion for those who are carrying the weight.

Spiritual care also matters. Caregivers may wrestle with questions of meaning, with anger at God, with guilt over not doing enough, with grief that begins long before death. Planning should include space for caregivers to have their own rituals, their own prayers, their own support networks. Clergy, counselors, and community groups can provide this, but families must make it a priority. To care for the caregiver spiritually is to strengthen them for the journey.

There is also the delicate balance of decision making. Caregivers are often the ones who must speak to doctors, who must weigh options, who must decide whether to continue treatments. These decisions can haunt them if they are made in uncertainty. Planning relieves this by giving clear instructions. Advance directives, written wishes, and conversations about values remove the burden of guesswork. A caregiver who knows exactly what their loved one wants can act with confidence rather than fear. They may still grieve, but they will not carry the heavy shadow of doubt.

Technology now plays a role as well. Digital planning tools can help families coordinate schedules, share updates, and track medications. Group chats, shared calendars, and online platforms can divide tasks more evenly. These tools are not replacements for love, but they are supports that can make caregiving more sustainable. Including them in the plan is a simple yet powerful way to ease the load.

Planning for caregivers also means preparing for what comes after. When the loved one dies, caregivers often feel lost. They have devoted months or years to a role that suddenly disappears. The silence can be devastating. They may also feel resentment that others can return to normal life while they are left with exhaustion and grief. Anticipating this transition is important. Families can plan to surround the caregiver after the death, to check on them, to invite them back into social life, to acknowledge their sacrifice. Without this, caregivers may feel abandoned at the very moment they most need connection.

I once met a man who had cared for his wife through a long illness. After she died, he said he felt not only widowed but unemployed, purposeless, erased. He had been her caregiver for so long that he no longer knew who he was without that role. Slowly, with the help of friends and community, he rebuilt his sense of self. But he told me he wished someone had prepared him for the emptiness. He wished the planning had included him not only as a caregiver but as a person who would need support afterward. His words remind us that caregiving does not end with death. It leaves ripples that must be tended.

Live Fully. Leave Wisely.

To plan for caregivers is, at its heart, to recognize that end of life care is a family affair. It is not only about the dying person. It is about everyone touched by the journey. By preparing for the caregiver, we affirm that their love is not to be taken for granted. We give them the gift of clarity, the gift of support, the gift of acknowledgment. We remind them that while they may carry much, they do not carry it alone.

When death comes, and it always does, the person who is leaving deserves dignity, love, and peace. But so too does the one who stays and cares. To plan for both is to embrace the fullness of love. It is to honor not only the ending of a life but the lives that are stretched, tested, and changed by the act of caregiving.

In the end, caregiving is one of the purest expressions of love. It is love made visible in actions, in patience, in presence. Planning for caregivers ensures that this love is not left unsupported, that it does not turn into silent suffering. It ensures that the caregiver, too, is carried. And perhaps that is the final lesson. In death, as in life, no one should walk alone.

Chapter

19

GREEN AND ALTERNATIVE BURIALS

For centuries, burial was simple. A body was returned to the earth, often in the most direct and natural way possible. Families dug graves with their own hands, built plain wooden coffins, and lowered their loved ones into the ground close to home. There was a humility in those burials, a closeness to the cycle of life and death. Over time, though, burial became more industrialized. Embalming, sealed caskets, metal vaults, manicured lawns, and rows of stone monuments turned cemeteries into carefully maintained landscapes. For some, these traditions brought comfort and dignity. For others, they felt sterile, expensive, and disconnected from the natural world.

In recent years, there has been a growing movement toward green and alternative burials. People are beginning to ask whether the way we bury the dead reflects not only love for the person but also care for the earth. They are asking whether embalming fluids, steel caskets, and concrete vaults are truly necessary. They are asking if there are gentler, simpler ways to say goodbye. The answers are beginning to reshape how we think about death itself.

I remember speaking with a woman whose husband had requested a green burial. She told me that at first she resisted the idea. She had grown up visiting cemeteries where polished headstones and neatly trimmed grass were the norm. She wondered if a green burial would feel too bare, too primitive. But after his death, she honored his wishes. His body was placed in a simple shroud and lowered into the earth in a meadow. Wildflowers grew above him, and birdsong filled the air. She told me that standing there, watching nature embrace him, she felt something unexpected. She felt peace. She said it was as if he had returned to the rhythm of the world, not set apart from it. What had seemed strange became beautiful.

The green burial movement rests on a simple truth: the body is part of nature. To embalm it with chemicals, to seal it away in metal, to surround it with concrete, is to resist the natural cycle. Green burials allow the body to decompose naturally, to nourish the soil, to become part of the earth again. For many, this feels not only environmentally responsible but spiritually meaningful. It is a way of saying that death is not an end but a return.

There are other forms of alternative burial that reflect this same spirit of creativity and care. Some families choose cremation and scatter ashes in meaningful places—a favorite hiking trail, the ocean, a mountaintop. Others plant ashes beneath a tree, allowing new life to grow from death. There are even biodegradable urns designed to nurture seeds, so that a loved one's remains can become part of a living forest.

Paul Fried

I once met a family who chose to place their mother's ashes inside a coral reef project. Her remains were mixed with environmentally safe concrete and lowered into the ocean, where they became part of an artificial reef. Fish swam around the structure, coral began to grow, and her children said they felt as though their mother had not only left them but had given something back to the earth. Her final act was to become part of the ocean she had loved all her life.

For some, alternative burial is about cost as much as meaning. Traditional funerals can be expensive, with caskets alone costing thousands of dollars. Green burials often cost less, since they avoid embalming, vaults, and elaborate coffins. For families struggling with finances, this can be a relief. Yet even for those who could afford more, many choose simplicity as an expression of values. They say I do not need grandeur. I need honesty. I need closeness to nature.

Not everyone is comfortable with these choices. Some see them as too unconventional, too far from tradition. Others worry that simplicity might look like neglect. But the truth is that alternative burials are not about doing less. They are about doing differently. They are about aligning death with beliefs about life, about the environment, about spirituality. For some, that alignment is more important than following convention.

Faith traditions sometimes intersect with these questions in unique ways. Jewish and Muslim practices, for example, already align with many principles of green burial. Bodies are washed, wrapped in simple shrouds, and buried quickly without embalming or elaborate coffins. The emphasis is on humility and returning to the earth. In many ways, these traditions anticipated what the green movement is rediscovering. Other traditions, like Catholicism, historically favored burial in consecrated ground but have adapted to accept cremation, though still with guidelines. In each case, families must navigate the balance between faith, tradition, and personal conviction.

I recall a young man who told me his father had wanted cremation, but his grandmother insisted on a full traditional burial. The family argued for days, torn between honoring the father's wishes and respecting the grandmother's faith. In the end they compromised, cremating him and then burying the ashes in the family plot. It was not perfect, but it was honest. It reflected both the man's personal choice and the family's cultural ties. That compromise is part of planning too—acknowledging that death affects not only the individual but the wider community.

Alternative burial practices also remind us that death can be creative. Some people design their own farewell in ways that feel unique and personal. I knew a woman who arranged for her ashes to be placed in a firework and launched into the sky. Her friends gathered, and when the rocket burst into colors, they laughed and cried at the same time. It was not traditional, but it was hers. It reflected her joy, her playfulness, her love of spectacle. It turned grief into celebration.

Others turn to art. Some companies now transform ashes into glass sculptures or jewelry. A daughter once showed me a necklace that held a small amount of her mother's ashes within a delicate blue stone. She said she wore it every day, not as a fashion piece but as a way of carrying her mother with her. For her, it was a daily reminder that love persists beyond death.

Of course, there are ethical debates around these practices. Some worry that they commercialize death too much, turning grief into another market. Others argue that any ritual, however unconventional, is meaningful if it comforts the living and honors the dead. These debates will continue, but they all point to the same underlying truth: death is no longer confined to one model. Families are seeking freedom, and that freedom is reshaping the landscape of how we say goodbye.

Green and alternative burials also challenge us to think about legacy. Do we want our last act on earth to leave behind chemicals, concrete, and cost—or do we want it to nourish, to give back, to reflect simplicity. This is not a question with one right answer. For some, a traditional headstone brings comfort and continuity. For others, a wildflower meadow feels like a truer reflection of their values. Planning is about making that choice intentionally, not leaving it to others to decide in confusion.

I remember walking through a natural burial ground once. There were no rows of polished granite, no rigid order. Instead there were meadows, trees, stones carved with simple names, wooden markers that would one day fade. Birds sang, the wind moved through tall grasses, and the place felt alive. It was not only a resting place for the dead but a living landscape for the living. Families wandered slowly, touching stones, leaving flowers, sitting quietly. It felt less like a cemetery and more like a continuation of life. That experience stays with me as a reminder that beauty in death does not always require grandeur. Sometimes it requires returning to the simplest truths of nature.

Green and alternative burials invite us to rethink what it means to honor someone. They ask whether love is measured in steel and stone or in presence and intention. They remind us that the earth is not only where we are buried but where we have lived. To return gently to it can be a final act of harmony.

In the end, choosing a green or alternative burial is not about rejecting tradition but about aligning death with values. It is about asking what feels authentic, what brings peace, what reflects the person who has died. It is about giving families the freedom to grieve in ways that resonate, whether through wildflowers, coral reefs, fireworks, or jewelry. Each choice tells a story. Each choice becomes part of legacy.

What matters most is not whether the burial is traditional or alternative, elaborate or simple. What matters is that it is chosen with love, with intention, with clarity. When that happens, the burial itself becomes more than a ritual. It becomes a final gift.

Chapter

20

YOUR LEGACY IN ACTION

We often think of legacy as something that happens after we are gone, as if it begins only when the last breath is taken and the obituary is written. But legacy is not a final chapter. It is being written every day, in the choices we make, in the words we speak, and in the silences we allow. Legacy is not waiting in the future like a sealed envelope. It is alive in the present, shaping how people know us, how they remember us, and how they carry our influence into their own lives.

I remember a man who told me he never thought much about legacy until he became a grandfather. He said that one afternoon he was sitting on the porch, watching his granddaughter play in the yard, and it struck him that she would carry his memory long after he was gone. He thought about what that memory might be. Would she remember him as kind and patient, or would she remember him as distracted and busy. He realized, in that moment, that legacy is not only what you leave in a will or what is written in a eulogy. It is the small gestures that add up to a story, the way you show up for people, the tone of your voice, the choices you make when no one is watching.

Legacy in action is the recognition that what you do today becomes tomorrow's memory. It is the way you treat the cashier at the grocery store, the way you listen when your child wants to tell you something that feels unimportant to you but matters deeply to them. It is whether you forgive a friend, whether you make time to call your parents, whether you take responsibility when you are wrong. These things may seem ordinary, but when they are repeated over years they become the narrative that others will tell about you.

One woman told me that her father never left her any money, property, or material wealth. What he left her instead was a habit of compassion. He volunteered every weekend at a local shelter, and when she was a child he brought her along. At the time she did not always appreciate it. She wanted to spend her Saturdays with friends, not serving meals to strangers. But years later, after he had passed, she realized that those Saturdays had formed the foundation of her own values. She now runs her own nonprofit, serving the same community where her father once stood beside her. She said his legacy was not in the bank but in her heart, and every act of service she performed felt like carrying his voice forward.

That is legacy in action. It is not static. It is not confined to a document or a gravestone. It breathes and moves in the lives of others long before and long after your death.

Yet many people wait too long to think about legacy. They imagine it as something to be considered in old age, when the will is written and the estate is organized. But legacy begins much earlier. It begins in how you raise children, how you mentor employees, how you respond to failure, how you celebrate success. It begins in the patterns you set and the lessons you teach without even realizing it.

I once spoke to a man who regretted never telling his son that he was proud of him. He assumed his son knew, because he provided for the family and showed up to his games. But he never said the words. When the man grew sick and knew his time was limited, he finally told his son, and the relief in both of their faces was overwhelming. He later told me that if he had learned one lesson, it was that legacy is not something to be implied. It must be spoken. It must be lived out loud.

The stories we leave behind are built on the stories we tell today. Think about how many families pass down traditions not through wealth but through repetition. A holiday meal cooked the same way every year, a phrase repeated so often it becomes part of the family language, a ritual of gathering that continues even after the originator is gone. These actions become the threads of legacy, weaving lives together.

There is a danger, though, in leaving legacy to chance. Silence has a way of writing its own story, often harsher than the one we intended. When we avoid conversations about values, when we avoid apologies, when we avoid preparation, we risk leaving behind confusion and bitterness. That too is a legacy, though not the one we would choose. I have met countless families who speak not of what their parent gave them but of what they withheld, a blessing never spoken, forgiveness never offered, guidance never given. Those silences echo just as loudly as words.

Legacy in action means choosing to be intentional. It means recognizing that you are shaping memory every day and asking whether the memory you are creating is the one you want to leave behind. It does not require wealth, fame, or extraordinary talent. It requires honesty, courage, and consistency.

Live Fully. Leave Wisely.

Consider the ripple effect of simple actions. A teacher encourages a student who doubts herself, and that student goes on to pursue a career she might never have attempted. Years later, she tells her own children about the teacher who believed in her, and they learn the importance of encouragement. One small act, one word of belief, creates a chain of influence that stretches across generations. That is legacy, alive and moving, long before the teacher's name is etched in stone.

Some people confuse legacy with reputation. Reputation is how people talk about you in the moment. Legacy is how they carry you when you are no longer present. Reputation can be temporary and fragile, swayed by gossip or circumstance. Legacy is deeper. It is rooted in truth, in the real impact of your choices. You cannot control reputation completely, but you can shape legacy through the consistency of your values.

I once attended the funeral of a man who had been well known in his community. He had awards, achievements, and recognition. But when people stood to speak, they did not talk about his titles or his accolades. They talked about the time he fixed a neighbor's fence, the way he always remembered birthdays, the laughter he brought to gatherings. His reputation had been impressive, but his legacy was intimate. It lived in the everyday kindness that had touched people's lives.

The question, then, is not whether you will leave a legacy. Everyone does. The question is what kind it will be. Will it be one of silence or one of expression. Will it be one of regret or one of intention. Will it be one of burden or one of blessing.

Legacy in action is about living today as if it already matters to tomorrow. It is about forgiving sooner, speaking more honestly, loving more openly. It is about recognizing that every conversation may one day be remembered, that every decision may ripple into the lives of people you may never meet.

This is where planning meets living. We often think of end-of-life planning as separate from daily life, but in truth they are inseparable. Writing down wishes, making decisions about care, organizing documents—these are not only acts of preparation for death. They are acts of clarity in life. They tell your family who you are, what you value, and how you love them. They are part of legacy, already in action.

I remember meeting a woman who had written letters to each of her grandchildren before she died. She sealed them in envelopes to be opened on milestones—their sixteenth birthdays, their graduations, their weddings. She died before some of those events arrived, but her words were waiting. When her granddaughter graduated from college, she opened her letter and read her grandmother's encouragement, written years before. She told me it felt like her grandmother was sitting beside her, proud and present. That is legacy in action—love that transcends time.

You do not need to write letters or make grand gestures for your legacy to live. Sometimes it is as simple as showing up. A father who comes home tired from work but still makes time to play with his children is shaping memory. A friend who answers the phone at midnight when someone is in crisis is shaping memory. A leader who admits a mistake instead of hiding it is shaping memory. These choices are not dramatic, but they build the story that will be told long after the details of daily life fade.

There is a story I will never forget about a man who had been estranged from his brother for years. They fought over money, pride, and misunderstandings. When the man became ill, he realized that the bitterness was part of his legacy, and he did not want that to be his final gift. He called his brother, apologized, and reconciled. They spent the last months of his life together, repairing what had been broken. After his death, his brother told me that those months meant more than all the years of silence combined. The man's legacy shifted not through wealth or achievement but through humility and forgiveness. That, too, is legacy in action.

The truth is that we cannot control everything about how we are remembered. People interpret our lives through their own experiences and emotions. But we can shape the foundation. We can decide what values we live by, what love we express, what clarity we provide. We can choose whether our absence will be filled with confusion or comfort.

In this way, legacy is both a gift to others and a responsibility to ourselves. It challenges us to live authentically, to align our daily choices with the story we want told. It asks us to be courageous enough to face death not as an end but as a mirror that reflects how we have lived.

And here is the beauty of legacy in action: it is never too late to begin. Even one act of honesty, one conversation of forgiveness, one expression of love can ripple outward and transform the story. A man who lived selfishly for decades but chose kindness at the end is still remembered for that kindness. A woman who remained silent for years but finally spoke her heart to her children is still remembered for that courage. Legacy is not fixed until the final chapter is closed. Until then, every day is an opportunity to write.

So if you are reading this and wondering what your legacy will be, begin now. Speak the words you have been holding back. Reach out to the person you miss. Write down your wishes. Tell the stories you want remembered. Do not wait for later, because later has a way of vanishing.

Your legacy is not only what you leave behind when you die. It is what you live right now. It is in the hug you give, the apology you make, the laughter you share, the time you spend, the presence you offer. It is in the way you choose to show up for life.

That is legacy in action. That is the story you are writing, today and every day, whether you acknowledge it or not.

And when the time comes, when your voice is silent and others gather to remember, what they carry with them will not be the titles, the possessions, or the accolades. They will carry the memory of how you made them feel, the clarity of the love you showed, and the peace of knowing you lived with intention.

That is the gift of legacy in action. It is not about being remembered forever. It is about being remembered well.

Chapter

21

THE BEGINNING OF LEGACY

From the very first page of this book, we have been circling around the truth that most of us spend our lives trying to avoid. Death is real, and it is coming for each of us. We whisper about it, hide it behind euphemisms, and push it into the background of our busy days. Yet the more we avoid it, the heavier it becomes, casting shadows over families who are unprepared, straining relationships under the weight of silence, and leaving chaos in the very place where clarity should have been.

The chapters before this one have walked us through the ways avoidance harms us and the ways preparation frees us. We have faced the silence around death and grief. We have looked at the illusion of control and the urgency of legacy. We have considered the ways advance directives and wills protect the ones we love, and we have acknowledged the dignity that comes from making choices before someone else must make them for us. Each story, each reflection, each step has carried us further from denial and closer to responsibility.

But the truth is that this journey does not end with the signing of a document or the completion of a plan. Those things are essential, and they are acts of profound love. Yet they are not the whole story. They protect your family when you are gone, but they do not define how you will be remembered while you are still alive. That is the work of legacy.

Legacy is not waiting at the end of your life like an unmarked grave. Legacy is being written right now. It is in the conversations you have with your children, in the values you model for your friends, in the way you treat the people who pass through your daily orbit. Every moment adds another thread to the tapestry of memory, and those threads will one day outlive you.

This is why preparing for death is not only about death at all. It is about living with intention. When you decide where you want to die, how you want to be treated, what you want said at your funeral, you are not only sparing others confusion. You are shaping a story that reflects who you are and what you value. That story will echo in the lives of others long after you are gone.

I think of the woman who left letters for each of her grandchildren to open at milestones she knew she would never see. I think of the man who finally told his son he was proud, after a lifetime of leaving it unsaid. I think of families who were given clarity in their darkest moments, who could grieve without the added burden of uncertainty. These were not grand gestures of wealth or fame. They were simple acts of love that became legacies in themselves.

And this is where we turn the page. Because if this book has been about facing death with courage and making the arrangements that protect those we love, then the next step is something even larger. It is the conscious shaping of legacy. It is the recognition that while plans may end with your life, legacy begins with how you live every day you have left.

The conversation about legacy is deeper than paperwork. It asks harder questions. What will people say about you when you are gone. What traditions will continue because of you. What values will ripple forward through generations. What love will endure beyond your absence. These questions do not wait until the last chapter of life to be answered. They are answered now, in real time, with every choice you make.

There is freedom in realizing this. Legacy is not a burden that rests only on your final years. It is an invitation to live differently today. It is the reason to say the words you have been holding back, to repair the relationship you have neglected, to share the stories that your children and grandchildren may never otherwise hear. It is the reason to forgive more quickly, to risk more boldly, to love more openly.

So let this closing chapter not feel like an ending but like a beginning. You have faced what most people spend their lives avoiding. You have looked death in the eye and chosen preparation over silence. That choice is an act of love, one that will protect and comfort those you care about most. Now the invitation is to go further, to move from preparation into legacy, from making arrangements into making meaning.

The book in your hands was never only about dying wisely. It has always been about living fully. And living fully means recognizing that your story does not end with your death. It continues in the lives of others, in the memories they carry, in the love you gave, in the clarity you left behind.

This is where our journey together pauses, not because the subject is complete, but because a new horizon awaits. In the chapters of another book, we will dive more deeply into the heart of legacy, into how to craft it, live it, and pass it forward with courage and grace. For now, let this be your charge: begin today. Speak what matters. Write it down. Live with the urgency of one who knows that time is precious. Do not wait for tomorrow, because tomorrow is never guaranteed.

The plans you make may end with your life, but your legacy begins with how you live. Let that truth guide you, inspire you, and free you. This is not the end of the story. It is the beginning of your legacy.

The Final Word

At the end of the day, death will come for all of us. The business of death will always be there, ready to sell convenience and soothe uncertainty at a steep price.

But you don't have to play that game.

Planning ahead takes death out of the hands of strangers and puts it back where it belongs: with you, and with the people you love.

Because planning isn't about beating the system. It's about protecting your family. It's about leaving behind peace, not paperwork. Love, not debt. Clarity, not chaos.

If there's one message I want this book to leave you with, it's this:

Live Fully. Leave Wisely.

Death is inevitable. Chaos is optional.

You don't get to choose the day, the hour, or the way. But you do get to choose what you leave behind:

- A mess, or a map.
- Silence, or clarity.
- Burden, or love.

That choice is yours.

And the moment you take even one step, one note, one wish, one conversation, you've already begun to transform the business of death into the legacy of life.

That's planning. That's love in action. That's the gift you leave behind.

EPILOGUE

A Plan for Everyone

If you've made it this far, you know this book wasn't written to scare you. It wasn't written to depress you. It was written to free you.

We've walked through the hard truths together, how silence costs families, how planning lightens grief, how even the smallest steps can spare the people you love from chaos.

And here's the bottom line, this isn't about death. It's about love.

Love that speaks when you can't.
Love that gives clarity instead of confusion.
Love that carries forward long after you're gone.

That's the mission of **I Made the Arrangements** and the work we're doing at www.imadethearrangements.com to make sure no family is left scrambling in the dark, and that every person has a plan that reflects their life, their values, and their love.

I built IMTA because I've seen what happens when families are unprepared. I've watched grief get buried under debt, under paperwork, under fights that never should have happened. And I've also seen the peace that comes when a plan exists, even a simple one.

My mission is simple, **to see that everyone has a plan.**

Not just the wealthy. Not just the elderly. Not just the "organized." Everyone. Because everyone who loves someone, or owns something, needs one.

So, here's my challenge to you, Don't let this book just be something you read. Let it be something you *do*.

- Write one note.
- Have one conversation.
- Share one decision.

And when you're ready to go further, use the tools at www.imadethearrangements.com

They're built to walk with you step by step, to make planning simple, clear, and human.

You don't have to finish everything today. You just have to start.

Because when you do, you won't just change the story of your death. You'll change the story of your life, and the legacy you leave behind.

Death is inevitable. Chaos is optional. And love, written down, is forever.

ABOUT THE AUTHOR

Paul Fried is a serial entrepreneur, end-of-life planner, and founder of *I Made the Arrangements*, a human-centered platform that helps people prepare their wills, healthcare directives, funeral wishes, and legacies with clarity and compassion.

His path to this work is deeply personal. Paul is the son of Eugene Fried, a Holocaust survivor imprisoned at Auschwitz. His father carried the number A-4310 on his arm and the weight of memories that shaped every part of his family's life. Eugene lost his parents and two brothers to the gas chambers and endured sixteen-hour days in a coal mine. Growing up with that story gave Paul a profound awareness of life's fragility and the responsibility of carrying legacy forward.

Years later, Paul traveled to Auschwitz with his cousin Allan Brauner and walked through the camps where his father was imprisoned. The experience left a permanent mark. He came to understand more deeply that legacy is not a luxury or an afterthought. It is the thread that connects one generation to the next, and if it is not preserved intentionally, it can be lost to silence. His father's survival and testimony became the foundation of Paul's mission to ensure that stories, values, and love are never forgotten.

Paul Fried

As a father to his own children, Zach, Khira, and Leila, Paul began to reflect on what he would one day leave behind. He realized that while possessions and financial stability were important, they were not enough. What mattered even more were the stories, the clarity, and the peace of mind that could free his children from uncertainty and conflict. That desire to provide more than material inheritance became the seed of *I Made the Arrangements* and the inspiration for this book.

For the past two years, Paul has immersed himself fully in the subject of death, dying, and legacy. He has studied cultural practices and spiritual traditions, interviewed families, and worked alongside professionals in healthcare, law, and funeral care. He also trained as an end-of-life doula, helping individuals and families through the hardest of transitions with honesty and compassion. These writings are the culmination of that immersion, shaped by research, professional practice, and a lifetime of personal experience.

Paul believes that in our culture, death has been avoided for too long, hidden behind euphemisms and distractions. He has seen how avoidance only multiplies the suffering, while preparation creates clarity and peace. Through *I Made the Arrangements* and through this book, his mission is to replace avoidance with courage, silence with clarity, and chaos with love written down and preserved for those who remain.

Beyond this work, Paul has spent his professional life building businesses and taking risks. Entrepreneurship has always been a driving force in his life, but *I Made the Arrangements* is different. It is not just a business. It is his legacy project, born from his father's survival, his own reflections on mortality, and his love for his children.

Live Fully. Leave Wisely.

Paul lives in New Jersey where he enjoys good food, time with his family, and the ongoing work of helping people live fully and leave wisely. He believes death is inevitable, but chaos is not. He believes that love, when spoken and written, can endure beyond a lifetime.

www.ingramcontent.com/pod-product-compliance
Lightning Source LLC
Chambersburg PA
CBHW031646040426
42453CB00006B/223